Preschool Classroom Management

By Laverne Warner and Sharon Anne Lynch

Other books by Laverne Warner:

Fun With Familiar Tunes

Language in Centers: Kids Communicating

Themes Escapades: Learning Units for All Occasions

Tunes for Tots

What If Themes: Making the Most of Teachable Moments

Management

150 Teacher-Tested Techniques

Laverne Warner and
Sharon Anne Lynch

gryphon house, inc.
Beltsville, MD

Bulk purchase

Gryphon H███████████
for special ███████████
promotio ███████████
raising use. Special editions or book
excerpts also can be created to
specification. For details, contact
the Director of Marketing at
Gryphon House.

Disclaimer

Gryphon House, Inc. and the
authors cannot be held responsible
for damage, mishap, or injury
incurred during the use of or
because of activities in this book.
Appropriate and reasonable caution
and adult supervision of children
involved in activities and
corresponding to the age and
capability of each child involved, is
recommended at all times. Do not
leave children unattended at any
time. Observe safety and caution at
all times. Every effort has been
made to locate copyright and
permission information.

Copyright

Published by Gryphon House, Inc.
10726 Tucker Street, Beltsville, MD 20705
301.595.9500; 301.595.0051 (fax); 800.638.0928

Visit us on the web at www.gryphonhouse.com

Library of Congress Cataloging-in-Publication Data

Warner, Laverne, 1941-

Preschool classroom management : 150 teacher-tested techniques / by
Laverne Warner and Sharon Lynch.
    p. cm.
 Includes bibliographical references and index.
 ISBN 0-87659-291-4
 1. Classroom management. 2. Preschool education. I. Lynch, Sharon,
1949- II. Title.
 LB3013.L96 2004
 372.1102'4--dc22

                                  2004002096

Table of Contents

Section 2

Introduction

Mrs. Black overheard four-year-old T. J. say to Jeremy, "What would happen if I pulled that handle?" She heard Jeremy's reply, too, "I don't think you're supposed to do that," and she turned around in time to see T. J. pull the fire alarm in the foyer of their building that led to the playground. Within minutes the center was evacuated, and within hours Mrs. Black's director had ordered a protective cover installed over the alarm to prevent a similar event from happening again in their school.

Preschool Classroom Management: 150 Teacher-Tested Techniques is designed to assist teachers who are new to the field of early education or who have years of experience. It provides both a classroom management framework and solutions and suggestions of what to do when specific situations arise. Just like the protective cover placed over the fire alarm in the above anecdote, classroom management techniques described in this book aim to prevent problems before they happen or to provide solutions when they do.

Classroom management is a key component in helping children develop into independent individuals who can control their emotions, make positive decisions about their activities, and learn effectively. Classroom management provides a foundation for children as they learn socially appropriate behaviors. It is a process that requires interactions among teachers, parents, and children to help children understand their own feelings and the feelings of others. Positive interactions and relationships between children and adults are critical to children's successful learning.

The techniques described in this book are based on three beliefs:

1. Adults must model self-regulated behavior in their relationships with children.
2. Teachers need to be sensitive to children's needs.
3. Children want to know how to behave and to do what is expected of them.

Understanding these beliefs is important to the goals for children's development and learning. Teaching socially appropriate behavior is the most important component in classroom management.

How does this happen? Initially, *you need to have realistic expectations about the children you are assigned to teach.* Young children are generally impulsive, and emotional outbursts are typical during their waking hours. They cry, push, shove, yell, want toys others have, and they live in the moment. As Joanne Hendrick (2003) writes, "…children's wants are immediate, intense, and personal" (p. 249). Daily interactions with young children require you to be responsive to children's needs and approach classroom management with calmness and consistency.

Children need adults who are concerned about them and who understand that the problems they are encountering are real. You must be willing to help children find solutions to their problems. Defining the problem and suggesting solutions that are workable will help children learn that life's problems, no matter how insurmountable they seem, can be discussed and eventually resolved.

Secondly, *you need to help children clarify the rules and limits they want to set within their classroom.* Five-year-olds are capable of helping to develop class rules, but younger children will most likely need the rules outlined for them. Three or four simple rules that cover a number of management areas are better than numerous, quite explicit statements. Children can learn to:

1) be a friend in the classroom
2) remember to take turns
3) think about safety

Taking time at the beginning of the school year to define the rules, and reminding children of the rules on a regular basis fall under the classroom management "umbrella." For example, Wilson's attempt to knock down Vergie's block structure could prompt the teacher to step in, remind Wilson that he needs to "be a friend" to Vergie, and talk with him about other activities he could do while waiting for Vergie to finish playing in the block center. Teachers use this strategy, known as *redirecting behavior* to maintain happy, productive classroom environments. The ability to utilize redirection effectively requires that teachers talk to children about their actions and help them understand the consequences of their behaviors.

"Look at Vergie," you might say. "She is upset that you knocked down her block structure. Wilson, let's help her pick up the blocks. Then I'll help you find something else to do for a while. Vergie will be through playing with the blocks later on, and then you can build your own block structure."

Sometimes you can help children by allowing them to work out their own problems. Attune your ears to what is happening, listening to hear whether children may be demonstrating that they are learning to assert their own needs without having to step in. For example, a loud yell from a child in the housekeeping center does not necessarily mean that immediate intervention is necessary. What you might hear, if you pause and listen, is this:

"Hey, Junie, you took my doll!" yells Marcy. "I wasn't through playing with it yet."

"I wanted to play with her today," asserts Junie.

"You can play with her in a minute. I wanted to feed her, but you can have her after that."

"Okay," Junie replies. "I'll be back to play with her when you finish feeding her."

The chapters in this book address a range of classroom management issues. Chapter 1 summarizes the behaviors effective teachers demonstrate when guiding young children, including how teachers can care for themselves and balance their own lives to work efficiently with children. Chapter 2 defines general classroom management principles that work in any classroom. The impact of environmental design and how it affects children's learning are addressed in Chapter 3 of this book. Planning effective daily routines and schedules is the topic of Chapter 4, developing a caring community of learners is the main theme of Chapter 5, and creating supportive parent partnerships is discussed in Chapter 6. Chapter 7 outlines analyzing problem behaviors, and Chapters 8 and 9 cover teaching alternative behaviors and communication skills. Classroom management, which is an ongoing process, is not always easy. Children need consistency. Lots of patience and numerous interactions with children and their parents are essential ingredients of effective classroom management.

Keep in mind the following as you use this book. First and foremost, none of the chapters of this book can be used alone as a complete guidance plan in any classroom. The described tips work only as well as your understanding of classroom management processes. Following the guidelines in all of the chapters will ensure that management problems will be minimal and workable solutions are within reach.

Managing behavior is, in fact, the development of a relationship with children. When teachers care for children, and their kindness and empathy are clear to children, then children will respond accordingly. When addressing a behavioral issue, it should be clear to children that you are trying to help them develop appropriate social skills and be better adjusted in the classroom. Guidance is teaching, and it is just as important as teaching about numbers, letters, and colors.

Second, children, like adults, have bad days and good days. The difference in children's reactions and those of adults is that adults are able to express their difficulties. Children do not always have the words to say, "I'm upset, so please excuse my bad behavior today." They need, instead, adults who can teach them the language they need as well as alternative behaviors that are more acceptable to others.

Bredekamp and Copple (1997) define effective teachers as ones who "listen and acknowledge feelings and frustrations, respond with respect, guide children to resolve conflicts, and model skills that help to solve their own problems" (p. 19). While no single book can define the answer to every management problem that will occur in a classroom, *Preschool Classroom Management* helps teachers analyze their own classroom situations and arrive at appropriate solutions to help develop self-managed young children.

Perhaps the most important point of *Preschool Classroom Management* is that having a positive attitude is a strong and desirable component of successful classroom management. If teachers believe children's behavior will change, then change will occur. If teachers believe that parents will respond to suggestions and recommendations, change will occur. If teachers view children's behavior as another aspect of children's growth and development, then their efforts to teach children positive behaviors will show results.

Most of all, when you work with children you need to be consistent, considerate, and in charge of yourself. If you demonstrate self-control and kindness, you will model behavior that children will want to follow.

Successful Teachers

**Chapter
1**

Mrs. Campbell has a spring in her step as she walks down the hall to her classroom. "Good morning," she smiles to fellow teachers. She almost skips into her classroom, which she spent a week decorating to be ready for her new group of four-year-olds. She smiles to herself as she unloads the new books she has brought to share with her group today.

"I'm ready!" she announces, cheerfully.

Why are some teachers happier with the teaching profession than others? Why are some people excited and eager to teach classrooms full of children? Why do others dread going to work and wonder why they ever believed they would be effective teachers? These questions are complex, but perhaps the following pages will shed light on the possible answers.

Characteristics of Successful Teachers

The Issue

Why are some teachers more successful in developing well-managed classrooms? Are there characteristics that set successful teachers apart from others when they walk into a classroom of children? What personal characteristics are essential to developing a caring classroom of learners?

Overview

Optimistic teachers have classrooms filled with optimistic children who find activities they enjoy. Teachers who guide children throughout the learning process yield positive results, as children learn valuable skills and concepts.

Goals

◆ To define the qualities of effective teachers and provide appropriate management models in the classroom so children will have successful, enjoyable experiences

Solutions

Successful teachers share these characteristics:
◆ understand child development
◆ are patient
◆ possess a gentle demeanor
◆ recognize children's varying developmental timetables
◆ are willing to assist children when they need help
◆ take the time necessary to explain rules to children
◆ are able to communicate well with parents
◆ are self-confident and well organized
◆ plan interesting activities for children
◆ are fun-loving
◆ enjoy being around children
◆ model enthusiasm for learning
◆ understand children's physical and emotional limitations
◆ are physically active and are willing to get down on children's level
◆ know that being with children is hard work

Keys to Effective Classroom Management

◆ Classroom management is an ongoing process, not completed in one day, and requires patience.
◆ Guidance of young children has lifelong results and is accomplished by confident, caring adults.
◆ Some children will be more challenging than others, and teacher knowledge about child development will yield positive results.
◆ Teachers and children will have "bad" days occasionally. Teacher modeling helps children learn how to express their emotions.

Showing Respect for Children

The Issue

Making negative comments about children, yelling at them, or using sarcasm in the classroom demonstrates disrespect for children.

Overview

Children need the same respect that adults share with one another. If your relationships with children are positive and you show respect for their contributions and efforts in the classroom, preschoolers will develop a sense of initiative, which eventually leads to an "I can do it" approach to living.

Goal

◆ To foster respectful relationships with children

Solutions

"Do you want to see me turn into a big, ugly bear?" A teacher asked this question to a four-year-old boy one day. No wonder he stared at her with amazement as he wondered whether she could really accomplish such a feat. The teacher's goal in uttering such a disrespectful question was to instill fear into the child.

"Stop that behavior right now!" is equally disrespectful of children. Just telling children what not to do does not instruct them about appropriate behavior. Children need adults to take time to explain what inappropriate behavior they are demonstrating and what behavior is more appropriate.

Children need to be valued for who they are, not what they do. Showing children that you care for them is an indication of respect. Chiding children for inappropriate behavior causes feelings of low self-esteem, and children often believe that adults do not like them when they are punished. Being sensitive to who children are will create positive feelings between you and children while they are learning appropriate social skills.

Keys to Effective Classroom Management

◆ Children learn about their value in society through the interactions with the significant people in their lives (parents, siblings, teachers, neighbors, and so on).

◆ Children learn about democratic living and their abilities to contribute to society when they are respected.

Being Sensitive to Children's Needs

The Issue

Children are bundles of physical, emotional, social, intellectual, and creative energy. Sometimes this energy is acted out with wiggly, squirmy behavior that may be difficult to tolerate, especially when children are in groups.

Overview

Preschool children may not be able to display quiet, attentive behaviors when asked. Your plans for classroom activities must recognize the developmental needs of children. Helping children get along with each other and learn how to interact in an appropriate manner in the classroom sets a foundation for future academic success.

Goal

◆ To meet children's needs, so their behavior in the classroom is appropriate and conducive to learning

Solutions

Children's needs are similar to adults' needs in that all individuals require physical, social, emotional, and intellectual nurturing in order to thrive. Children have less understanding of their needs and they require more free choice about their activities. To translate the understanding of children's needs to classroom practice, follow these general principles:

◆ Plan for a variety of choices for children in the classroom (See Chapter 3, Organizing for Centers).
◆ Organize the schedule to include large chunks of time for play.
◆ Allow time for children to work individually with activities they choose.
◆ Encourage children to participate in group experiences.
◆ Recognize that children cannot sit still for long periods of time.
◆ Provide materials for creative expression.
◆ Develop spaces that allow for children's private time.
◆ Plan for indoor and outdoor play.
◆ Remember that children need water and food throughout the daily schedule.
◆ Schedule rest times for children.

Keys to Effective Classroom Management

◆ Do not set unobtainable standards of behavior for young children. Occasionally examine your rules and allow children more freedom to make decisions for themselves.
◆ Children are novices in social settings—spend a great deal of time teaching children how to negotiate to get what they want.
◆ Children need constant reminders of classroom rules and how to conduct themselves when interacting with others.

Understanding Cultural Differences

The Issue

Adults' values systems vary from culture to culture based on experiences they had as children. Expectations of children's participation and contributions to group learning will also vary.

Overview

For example, if you take a teaching position in a predominantly Hispanic neighborhood and you have no knowledge or understanding of Hispanic culture, your expectations about children's learning or prior experiences may be different than the parents of the children in your care. Recognizing cultural differences will improve your ability to conference with parents and plan appropriate activities for the children in your classroom. Your understanding of children's cultural backgrounds sets the stage for positive school/home interactions.

Goal

◆ To make children feel comfortable when they recognize that their family and culture are respected within the school setting

Solutions

No matter the setting, your understanding of the children you teach will maximize their opportunities for learning. Children learn best when the educational experiences they receive are meaningful and relevant. Here are some helpful guidelines:

◆ Make many connections to a child's home life and what happens in the family setting.

◆ Identify and discuss special celebrations and neighborhood events children know about and participate in.

◆ Invite parents and neighborhood leaders to be vitally involved with school happenings.

◆ Collect artifacts for displays that are representative of the cultures in the class group.

◆ Sing songs and play games that connect to children's cultures.

◆ Display pictures of a variety of cultural groups, not only those cultures that are represented in the class.

◆ If children speak other languages, learn a few key phrases in their language to use when the children arrive on the first day.

◆ In addition, learn words or phrases that will help you understand children when they communicate their physical needs (such as going to the bathroom or obtaining food or water). Some suggestions are:

　　¿Habla español? (Do you speak Spanish?)
　　¿Necesite vaya a la baño? (Do you need to go to the bathroom?)
　　Vamos a la baño. (Let's go to the bathroom.)
　　¿Qué usted necesite? (What do you need?)

◆ Talk to your administrator about planning and implementing all-school festivals and programs that include family participation.

Keys to Effective Classroom Management

◆ Some families may mistrust schools and may not realize the importance of becoming a part of school life. With the help and support of the administration, take the initiative to establish a relationship with families of the children in your classroom.

Learning From Mistakes

The Issue

Franklin's outburst startled the teacher and all the children in the classroom. His teacher was afraid that he had seriously hurt himself until she discovered that his cries were because he had spilled a jar of paint on the floor.

Overview

Children make mistakes from time to time. When you react positively, children learn positive attitudes about their accidents and mishaps.

Goal

◆ To help children recognize that mistakes are a part of daily living, so that when they grow up, they will be less likely to berate themselves and feel helpless

Solutions

"Don't cry over spilt milk" is a popular cultural adage. Children can learn this concept during their early years. Humans make mistakes, and how we view our errors is important to our success in life. Consider these guidelines when mistakes happen:

◆ Remain calm when children drop objects or break items.

◆ React with concern when children hurt themselves (or others).

◆ If children are young preschoolers, help them clean up their messes.

◆ If children are older preschoolers, give them an opportunity to pick up after themselves.

◆ Use positive comments such as, "It's okay, Franklin, everyone makes mistakes," or "Let's clean up this spill, so others won't get paint on themselves."

◆ Enlist other children's assistance to clean up spills and clutter, because doing so teaches them about helping others.

◆ Model positive attitudes toward your own mistakes. A comment such as, "Oops, I made a mistake; let me correct it" shows children that mistakes are part of life.

Keys to Effective Classroom Management

◆ View your own mistakes positively. Taking responsibility for mistakes and correcting the problem models appropriate behaviors for children.

Modeling Appropriate Behavior for Children

The Issue

Ms. Chester noticed that a group of her children were playing in the home living center. She overheard Marisa yell to the others, "Stop that right now. You're in big trouble, and I'm going to whip your butt!"

Overview

Children observe and imitate adults when learning about social relationships and establishing relationships with others. You can model and teach children appropriate social behaviors.

Goal

- To create a harmonious classroom using consistent instructions

Solutions

Successful teachers demonstrate these classroom behaviors:

- Show kindness towards others
- Show sympathy to others when they are hurt or upset
- Ask for items instead of taking them
- Greet visitors when they enter the room
- Help new children learn the routines and layout of the classroom
- Take turns at the water fountain or with playground and classroom equipment
- Show how to sit on the floor with legs crossed
- Stand in a line or in a group with other children
- Enter a play setting without disrupting the engaged children
- Explain routines associated with eating lunch and after-lunch cleanup activity
- Clean up an area before leaving it, such as a classroom center
- Explain how to dispose of trash
- Show how to hold pencils, markers, and crayons
- Prepare the classroom for dismissal

Children want to be socially appropriate, so model for children what they need to do to work and play successfully in the classroom. If you work with young preschoolers, be aware that they might not have prior knowledge about appropriate classroom behaviors.

You may need to provide individual instruction if specific children do not grasp the basic principles of sitting or working together in a group. Taking children aside and explaining the expectation of group behaviors may be necessary to help them accomplish socially acceptable behavior.

Keys to Effective Classroom Management

- Interventions are often essential in helping children learn new behaviors, which takes time, patience, and consistency.
- As children mature, they continue to learn about social expectations. What is expected of three-year-olds is different from expectations of kindergartners, so adjust your instructions and modeling to match the needs of the learners in your classroom.

Nurturing Personalities

The Issue

Young children are in the process of learning to control their emotions. As their teacher, you will nurture and support children on many occasions throughout their time in the classroom.

Overview

Learning to be independent and managing one's problems requires adult guidance throughout children's growing years. Children need teachers who feel comfortable holding and soothing children when their feelings erupt.

Goal

◆ To help children understand that each of us faces problems, that they can be tackled (and, hopefully, solved), and that, occasionally, some situations simply must be accepted

Solutions

Children have problems when:

they are hurt	Show tender loving care (TLC) and use first-aid supplies to assist children in dealing with their scrapes and scratches.
they are confused	Hold children close and talk to them gently to determine the source of their agony. This should provide information that you can use to help solve the issue that is bothering them.

Keys to Effective Classroom Management

◆ Help children approach problems realistically. Not all problems have easy solutions. Some problems are best dealt with when alternative activities keep children busy and involved.

they are frightened	Comfort them and talk with them about their fears to alleviate their fears (real or imagined).
they are victimized	When children attack others in the classroom, care for the victim first, expressing sympathy and determining whether the victim is physically harmed. Once the victim is cared for, then talk to the offender, pointing out the feelings of the victim and repeating class rules about caring for one another. (If the offender attacks others often, then you may need to take firmer action. See page 144 for information about working with challenging behaviors).
their families are in conflict	Children react in differing ways when their families are having problems. Sometimes youngsters become aggressive or they may withdraw from normal classroom activity. Often, the best step in helping children whose families are in conflict is to talk to parents. Approaching children becomes easier if you understand the problems they are facing.
a member of their family dies	Children's comprehension of death is unlike adult understanding until they are about age nine. If children experience the death of a parent, learning to live with the death will take time (and, occasionally, professional intervention). Talk to children about death in a straightforward and sensitive way, and keep the conversation ongoing until the child has worked through the grief process.
they experience separation	When their parents leave them (even for a short period of time), tell children that their loved one will return (if possible, be specific about a timeframe—after nap time, as an example). Engage children in an activity, such as drawing a picture for their mother or father or writing a letter to them.

Recognizing Inappropriate Behavior

The Issue

What you view as inappropriate behavior may not be viewed in the same way by another teacher.

Overview

Negative behavior is affected by a number of variables:

◆ the specific setting where the behavior occurs;

◆ what behaviors the child has exhibited during the day (or week);

◆ the relationship the adult has with the child;

◆ what other events are going on in the classroom at the time in question; and

◆ how the adult feels in the classroom on the day in question.

Goal

◆ To recognize milestones in growth and development to determine how best to handle a problem that occurs in your classroom

Solutions

Your value system affects your beliefs about what is appropriate behavior and what is not. For example, a child who openly masturbates in the classroom may upset one adult, while another adult may interpret masturbation as a normal activity that is inherent in growth and development. Attending workshops and reading journals and books about child development is essential to learning what is appropriate behavior for the age levels of children you teach.

Often, children need simple explanations about their behaviors to teach them what is "right" or "wrong" in the classroom. Children who use curse words or inappropriate language at home will use them in the school setting, too. Explaining to children that this language is "not appropriate in our classroom" gives them a reason for eliminating the bad language. Telling them which words to use helps them learn the appropriate terminology to substitute.

Additionally, the age of the child will determine whether a behavior is appropriate or not. An emotional outcry from a child who is three is normal, but a similar outcry from a seven-year-old is not. In either case, teachers need to investigate the cause of the outburst and tell children that words are easier to understand than screams. Once the cause is determined, teachers have a number of options for helping the child resolve the problem.

Keys to Effective Classroom Management

◆ Look at a child's overall development and interactions within the classroom before making a judgment about what is appropriate behavior. For example, a child who masturbates at age three is within the norm of self-exploration for her age. A child who openly masturbates at age six may be indicating a serious problem within her family or delayed social/emotional development (Hendrick, 2002).

◆ Children need adults who view them as basically good people and accept them unconditionally.

Children Who Have Strong Emotions

The Issue

"I hate you," one child screams as he attacks his teacher. This tantrum is typical of others he has demonstrated in the classroom. His vehemence and anger are bursts of hurt and pain that the child has felt in his own life.

Overview

Children live what they feel and what they may have observed in other situations. When children yell obscenities or angry slurs toward adults, they are responding in ways that have given them attention, whether negative or not. Teaching children about appropriate reactions to situations that anger them is important to their development into adulthood. Through time, children will learn to talk about their anger and learn to solve their own problems.

Goal

◆ To give children positive behavior role models

Solutions

How you respond to situations will teach an angry child about controlling his emotions. Although positive reactions are difficult to model, they are essential in helping children learn to control their emotions. The steps to follow when a child is uncontrollable are as follows:

◆ Remove the child from the setting that is frustrating him.
◆ Calm the child as quickly as possible. Sometimes it will be necessary to allow him to kick and scream until he calms himself.
◆ Talk to him about the negative consequences of his behavior. For example, say, "Your classroom friends don't like to see you behave inappropriately when you're at school" or "Everyone gets angry sometimes, but talking about your anger is better than hurting yourself or others." This assists the child in imagining the behavior from the viewpoint of others.
◆ When the child is calm, tell him about appropriate expressions of anger. Say, "We don't know why you're angry when you throw a tantrum. Tell us about your anger, so it will be easier for us to find a solution to your problem."
◆ Help the child return to his rightful spot in the classroom. Let him know that adults are available to assist him when he's having problems.
◆ Continue to monitor the child. Encourage him when he is showing positive behaviors, and compliment his positive return to classroom activity.

Keys to Effective Classroom Management

◆ Intervention into children's negative cycles of behavior takes time, patience, and continued support from adults. With adult guidance, they can break the negative cycle and also learn to forgive others.

Keeping a Positive Attitude About Classroom Management

The Issue

After teaching for many years, teachers sometimes lose the spontaneity and joy of being with children day in and day out. They may start viewing children's behavior as spiteful or vengeful. They can become negative in their relationships with children (and sometimes, with their peers).

Overview

Working with children on a daily basis is a challenging job that is tiring and not always appreciated. At the end of a week that has presented more than its share of challenges, you may lose patience and understanding. Negativity builds upon negativity, and positive attitudes are lost.

Goal

- To work through periods of negativity when they arise. If negative feelings continue, you may need to re-evaluate whether you are in the profession that is right for you.

Solutions

Telltale signs that you are becoming negative occur in and out of the classroom. If you regularly complain about the children (or even about their parents), you need rest and relaxation. Getting away from children, even for a short period of time, will be beneficial. Try a few of these "emotional getaways" that are guaranteed to lift the spirits:

- Plan a trip to the gym. Have an invigorating workout.
- Take a trip to visit an old friend.
- If necessary, take a day off (called "mental health" days by experienced teachers).
- Call friends you haven't talked to for a long time.
- Read an uplifting book (something spiritual is helpful).
- Buy a new item of clothing. An inexpensive piece of costume jewelry may be all you need.
- If negative feelings persist, consider professional help from a counselor or psychologist.

When you're in the classroom, try these tips for looking at life more positively:

- Count your blessings. There are probably 16 little ones right in front of you!
- Plan activities in the classroom that will help get you in touch with the children's emotions. Ones you have enjoyed from the past are generally more effective than trying new experiences.
- Talk to children about feelings. Tell them that all of us have negative feelings periodically. Help them brainstorm ideas for becoming more positive. Try some of their suggestions.
- Remember that developing positive relationships with young children is the most important element in teaching. Focus on who the children are, not what they need to know in order to achieve.

Keys to Effective Classroom Management

- Teacher behaviors and coping skills influence children, who need positive models to learn the value of living each day to the fullest.

Enjoying Children

The Issue

You have unique talents that provide the stamina, energy, and fortitude to become a leader in your classroom. Yet, you feel that something is missing.

Overview

The teaching process requires two components:

♦ children who want guidance from adults; and

♦ adults who enjoy children. When adults enjoy what they do, children benefit.

Goal

♦ To remind teachers that the relationship they establish with children is critical to the learning process

Solutions

Being a teacher places demands on you. However, remembering to enjoy children will facilitate the relationship you have with them and prevent you from "burning out." Try these ideas for developing better relationships with children.

♦ Get to know the child's family.

♦ Find out what out-of-school activities children do with their families.

♦ Remember children's birthdays.

♦ Celebrate the birth of children's siblings.

♦ Greet children personally as they arrive each morning.

♦ Post children's family pictures in the classroom.

♦ Send notes home to parents or guardians about children's accomplishments.

♦ Encourage parents to become a part of the life of the school.

♦ Talk to your director about having regularly scheduled family nights.

♦ Laugh with children whenever possible.

Keys to Effective Classroom Management

♦ The key ingredient to becoming a successful teacher of young children is the enjoyment of children.

Enthusiasm for Learning

The Issue

When children seem bored and uninterested in normal activities, they need something new to interest them. Teachers who possess enthusiasm for learning will provide the spark that opens new avenues to knowledge.

Overview

Classrooms can become dull if the same instructional materials, books, and classroom equipment are used in the classroom without adequate discussion about their use. Wholesale change is not necessary, either, because children appreciate familiarity and routine. Enthusiasm for learning implies that you know the difference between spicing up classroom learning and creating chaos with too much change.

Goal

◆ To spark children's renewed interest in classroom activities by demonstrating how materials and equipment may be used in new ways, or expressing an interest in new experiences and information

Solutions

How can you create enthusiasm for classroom activities? Try some of these suggestions:

◆ Add a few new toys or a set of puzzles that will challenge children.
◆ Create a bulletin board and encourage children to add their artwork.
◆ Do seasonal activities. For example, in autumn, start a collection of acorns or leaves that children can collect on the playground.
◆ Change a few books in the Book Corner to accompany a new thematic study or a change in the weather.
◆ Get a classroom pet.
◆ Introduce a new CD that develops spontaneous movement activity.
◆ Invite parents or other visitors into the classroom to share their various expertise areas.
◆ Tour the building and allow children to recite favorite fingerplays or sing songs to other groups of children.
◆ Investigate community resources that will bring in objects for children to learn about (animal shelters may bring in pets, for example, or high school students can bring in collections or books to read to children).
◆ Plan a special field day that encourages families' participation.
◆ Collaborate with another teacher to develop an activity that will be mutually beneficial to both groups of children (for example, older children reading to younger ones or a pen-pal program).
◆ Videotape or audiotape children occasionally for parent programs to be held later in the year.
◆ Plan a walking field trip to a site in the neighborhood.

Keys to Effective Classroom Management

◆ Planning a new unit of study for children when the previous one has run its course takes a little imagination and abundant energy, but the payoffs are delightful. Children's cheerful laughter and renewed enthusiasm for classroom activities will be wonderful music to your ears.

Keeping Balance in One's Life

The Issue

Having a well-balanced life is essential for any professional in order to maintain focus on the important aspects of one's job. Teachers, more than most professional groups, must keep their emotional lives in check to establish positive relationships with children.

Overview

Teachers, just like parents, have tremendous influence in children's lives. Adult negativity often emerges when teachers are not caring for their own emotional health. Finding personal time for oneself should be a part of every teacher's daily health regimen.

Goal

- To keep your life in balance, so you can provide a model of happiness and emotional health that will have a positive impact on who children become

Solutions

Finding time for oneself is difficult to do in contemporary living, especially if teachers have families or other responsibilities beyond the classroom. Rushing from work to home to meetings causes stress and anxiety, which occasionally erupt in physical illnesses or pains (headaches or stomachaches, as examples). Balancing one's life brings personal happiness. Here is a checklist of emotional areas that teachers need to monitor:

- Is my family life stable and consistent?
- Do I have a few good friends I can count on when my life is out of sorts?
- Is my ability to laugh and enjoyment of living "within the normal range"?
- Do I plan adequately to work well with children when they come to school?
- Do I smile when children come into the classroom?
- Does my classroom emulate my pleasure in teaching?
- Am I interested in the children's activities?
- Do I allow children an opportunity to talk to me during the school day?
- Do I express an interest in children's work when they show it to me?
- Am I sympathetic when children share unhappy news with me?
- Do I share information about my home life with children?
- Do I take time to broaden my understanding of my profession?
- Do I pursue projects and activities outside the classroom that bring me personal satisfaction?
- Do I exercise on a regular basis?
- Do I use common stress reduction techniques (deep breathing, stretching, or singing to myself) when I need them?
- Am I in touch with my spirituality?
- Do I know when I need a "time out" from the children? Do I take this time when I need it?

Keys to Effective Classroom Management

- Just stepping away from the children for a few minutes and taking deep breaths will eliminate undue pressure from exploding in inappropriate teacher behaviors. Children don't need to see a frustrated teacher!

Putting It Into Practice: Linda

The principles supporting this narrative are:

- Classroom management requires teachers to deal with individual problems.
- When one technique fails, try another.
- Some children respond quickly, while others require a longer time to respond.
- Involve the family as much as possible when dealing with a child's problems.
- Sharing personal experiences will facilitate children's understanding of their own problems.
- Children may need instruction about expressing their feelings before they can verbalize their needs and concerns.
- Professional assistance beyond the classroom is necessary on occasion.
- Patience and good humor are essential to success.

Mrs. Soose was concerned about Linda, because she didn't seem to be fitting into her kindergarten class very well. She knew the family, because Linda's brother, Milt, had been in her classroom two years ago. Linda had visited in the classroom on several occasions, and she seemed to be happy to be there with her mother and brother. But now, she appeared withdrawn and clung to her mother each morning when they arrived. She didn't cry when her mother disappeared, but she fretted for a while and took a great deal of time trying to decide how to play, and she never wanted to join the circle each morning.

Mrs. Soose used the following strategies to determine the source of Linda's unhappiness:

- She began greeting Linda personally each morning when she arrived with her mother. As soon as possible, she talked privately with Linda's mother to learn if something was going on in the home that was creating a problem for the family or for Linda specifically.
- She also began holding Linda's hand until she was able to choose what activity she wanted to participate in. She modeled the language Linda needed to join the other children who were already in the play setting.
- Prior to Circle Time, she gave Linda a preview of the plans she had made for group time. Linda began showing an interest in the book that would be read, and knowing something about its contents seemed to motivate her to join the children when Circle Time was announced.
- Each day, she took time to ask about her brother, Milt.

Three months passed before Mrs. Soose was able to note that Linda's behavior appeared to be more social. She was beginning to make several friends, and Jamie, who lived in the same neighborhood, became a close friend. By the end of kindergarten, Linda was ready to move to first grade with a sense of confidence.

General Principles

Chapter 2

Working in classrooms requires that teachers understand basic principles of behavior. Interactions between teachers and children are founded on simple understandings about human behavior, which have been proven through time.

Successful teachers recognize that:

- Children want to be well behaved.
- Children want to be accepted and respected.
- Children want to please adults.
- Children require instruction about acceptable classroom behaviors.
- Children need time to develop their autonomy and self-control.
- Children do not expect perfection from their teachers (or their parents).
- Children respond to gentleness and kindness.
- Children eventually learn that rules are designed for the overall good of the group.
- Children learn from their mistakes.

Catch Them Being "Good"

The Issue

Children want to do what is expected of them, but sometimes they learn that negative behavior warrants more attention from adults. Consequently, they exhibit "bad" behavior.

Overview

Children want to be recognized for positive behavior and feel appreciated by the adults in their lives. When teachers notice their positive behavior and comment about it, children respond with more positive behavior. Working with young children requires patience and time for acceptable behaviors to emerge and become routine with children.

Goal

◆ To help children learn to manage themselves in group settings and behave appropriately in social interactions

Solutions

Be aware of your relationships with children. Do you constantly chide children for things they do wrong? Setting a positive tone with classroom interactions solves many classroom problems before they happen. Consider the following:

◆ Observe children's behaviors and comment favorably when they exhibit behavior you want (sharing or turn-taking, as examples).

◆ Acknowledge group behaviors that show children demonstrating collaborative activity. Many times, a positive comment during play activities is sufficient.

◆ Praise, when awarded, needs to be sincere, not overly emotional or sentimental.

◆ Praise needs to be administered judiciously, especially at the beginning of the year. As children begin to understand and remember classroom rules, they need less praise and more acknowledgment that their behavior is acceptable. Often, smiles and nods of encouragement are all children need.

◆ When negative behaviors occur, correct them in private with the child or children involved.

◆ Children can learn to control themselves when given the appropriate information for correcting their own behavior and plenty of time to practice new or unfamiliar social skills.

◆ On occasion, ignoring inappropriate behavior (provided no one is getting hurt) will enable children to channel their energies toward more positive activities.

Keys to Effective Classroom Management

◆ Even on the best of days, young children will regress to immature behaviors when they are tired, hungry, angry, or upset.

◆ Becoming self-managed and independent is a process that takes some children a long time to achieve.

Ignoring Negative Behavior

The Issue

On occasion, children behave negatively to receive attention, even negative attention, from adults. Children who consistently behave negatively in the same ways probably are counting on teachers to respond with punishments that provide a "badge of honor" to the offending youngsters. Alert teachers will learn to ignore some behaviors and wait for appropriate responses they can compliment.

Overview

Praising good behavior and ignoring negative behavior (provided no one is getting hurt) is beneficial to children in the long term. Teachers can fall into negative patterns. For example, the children dilly-dally with the cleanup when they discover that the teacher will react in a dramatic way to their behavior. Such volatile emotional displays can be an interesting diversion to children, so they work to make them appear again. Soon the see-saw tug between children and teachers causes a negative reaction to occur again.

Goal

◆ To take control of your emotions and ignore the children's negative behavior, so a positive balance emerges

Solutions

Mrs. Sanderson's solution to behavior problems was to take a group of children to the director's office almost every day. Her colleagues would observe her daily trek down the hall and marvel at her almost-comedic comment that "these are my rowdy ones today!" The children seemed to relish their fate, and apparently they took turns being the "bad children of the day."

Finally, the director took Mrs. Sanderson aside and asked her if she were aware of her own behavior. Once the teacher became aware that she was part of the problem, her trips to the director's office became less frequent. Mrs. Sanderson learned to ignore the negative behavior (provided no one was getting hurt) that required daily punitive action on her part. By ignoring minor infractions and focusing on positive behavior, her children became "the 'good' children of the day."

Keys to Effective Classroom Management

◆ Ignoring negative behavior often takes but a minute or two of the teacher's time. Turning your back on minor negative behavior allows children the opportunity to take control of their own behaviors.

◆ If ignoring inappropriate behavior does not yield resolution, talk quietly and privately to the offending child, giving instructions about more acceptable behavior.

Addressing the Behavior, Not the Child

The Issue

When you handle behavior problems in the classroom, it is important to separate children from their behavior and address the behavior only. This approach is likely to be more successful in helping children change their behavior.

Overview

Preschool children are sensitive to how adults assess their behavior. They want to be liked, and they are often guilty when they have behaved negatively. To avoid producing guilt feelings in young children, address their behavior, not the whole child.

Goal

♦ To have children feel accepted as people when confronted with their negative behaviors, instead of feeling belittled

Solutions

The following are good examples of comments by teachers who value children, but must correct certain behaviors:

♦ "Lana, your talking during story time was a problem today. I know you forgot the rule about no talking during story time. How can we solve this problem tomorrow?"

♦ "Josh, you know I think you have many talents, including having strong muscles. But when you kick others in the classroom, you create problems for your friends and yourself. Let's talk about what you can do instead."

♦ "Just because you disobey the rules, Kirk, doesn't mean you're bad. What it means is that you've forgotten why we have rules. We have rules so we can have a happy classroom. Let me show you how to work with others in the Block Corner."

♦ "Jodie, you don't feel well today, do you? That makes you irritable and it appears you don't want to get along with your classmates. Come talk to me about what you are feeling."

In each of the above examples, the teacher is addressing the child's behavior, not the child.

Keys to Effective Classroom Management

♦ Teachers are human, so if you lash out in anger to children, apologize and tell them that you made a mistake.

Planning Ahead

The Issue

It's important to think through the consequences of an instruction. For example, if you say, "It's time to go outdoors to play," the children immediately rush to the exit. Indeed, it may be time to go outside and play, but you need a plan of action for getting the children ready to depart for the playground.

Overview

Your number one responsibility in a classroom is the safety of the children. Taking time to plan for changes in the schedule, for moving from one part of the building to another, and for transitions from school to home are critical components of each day.

Goal

- To keep children safe and orderly, because children are not always aware of impending dangers

Solutions

The following scenarios describe teachers who plan ahead:

- Ms. Motley's three-year-olds can be a handful, but she is enjoying working with each of them. She learned early in the school year that confusion erupts when she asks, "Do you want to hear this book again?" Some do, while others don't. Ms. Motley corrected this chaos by saying instead, "Let me read this book again."

- Mr. Larry has observed that his children are unaware that the street next to his school has a lot of traffic. Although there is a fence around the playground and the gate has a security latch, he is still concerned that one of his youngsters might wander into the street. He has talked with the director about providing a safety guard during outside playtime, and for arrival and dismissal times. He has suggested that the parents of the children may want to volunteer to provide this service.

- Mrs. Gilliam developed a system for collecting lunch money that saves her precious time each morning. When the children arrive at school, they drop their lunch money into an envelope that has their name on it and is attached to a poster on the classroom door. When children are engaged in classroom center experiences, Mrs. Gilliam is able to count the money without interruption.

- Ms. Jay knows that taking her children to the school library can be a challenge because it is a long walk. Her solution is that the librarian and her assigned aide meet the class halfway. This allows Ms. Jay to return to her classroom to organize for other events children have scheduled for the day.

Keys to Effective Classroom Management

- Before the school year starts, scrutinize the classroom and playground for impending dangers. Eliminate hazards, and before the children arrive, spend time thinking about how to keep them safe. For example, remove pieces of furniture that are worn and might break if sat on, or take away broken glass from the playground if it has become a dumping ground by thoughtless neighbors.

- Give children specific directions to minimize chaotic responses to classroom procedures.

Using Principles of Democratic Living

The Issue

Allowing children to participate in creating classroom procedures teaches them about democracy. On the other hand, using authoritarian procedures teaches them about obedience and conforming behavior by demanding compliance.

Overview

Teachers of young children have a responsibility to introduce democratic principles to children. Children will acquire these principles if you demonstrate democracy in action.

Goal

◆ To introduce democratic principles to children through teacher modeling

Solutions

How can you develop classroom democracy?

◆ Allow children to have choices whenever possible (do not suggest choices when choices do not exist).

◆ Give children freedom to participate in group decision-making experiences.

◆ Talk to children about what it means to get along together.

◆ Assign classroom duties to individual children, rotating their assignments weekly or bi-monthly.

◆ Encourage discussions about keeping the classroom environment healthy and clean.

◆ Refer to the classroom as "our home away from home."

◆ Discuss the responsibilities each child has to the overall classroom community.

- Privately remind individual children of classroom expectations when they demonstrate uncooperative behaviors.
- On occasion, hold classroom votes to decide which snack or drink will be served during snack time.
- Encourage children to develop a class logo or flag and work together to complete it.

Keys to Effective Classroom Management

- In addition to developing a sense of community in the classroom, older preschoolers will enjoy learning about their city's government. Draw parallels to the government procedures and their classroom routines and activities.

Setting Class Rules

The Issue

As the school director walked down the hall, she knew immediately that Mrs. Frazier was having difficulty with her class. The children were loud, and when she peeked into the classroom, she noticed that they seemed rowdy and unruly. "I need to talk to Alvena this afternoon," she thought to herself. "There doesn't seem to be any sense of classroom rules."

Overview

Effective classroom management is founded on the development of class rules. Children need to know and understand the rules, and to the degree possible, participate in their formation. Class rules should also be posted in the classroom so you and children can refer to them when necessary. Some schools adopt uniform rules that all children follow throughout their years in the school.

Goal

◆ To take time to communicate the classroom rules and to ask children for their cooperation in remembering and following the rules, so the classroom is well managed and children demonstrate appropriate behaviors

Solutions

From the first day children arrive, they need to know what behaviors are expected, and you need to communicate your expectations to the children. A few simple, positively worded, straightforward rules are best. By posting them on a chart in the classroom, you can refer to them when infractions occur.

If possible, give children an opportunity to participate in making the rules. When youngsters have a hand in forming the rules, they seem to remember them with greater ease. When a rule is broken, you can say, "Remember, we made this rule at the beginning of the school year. We agreed that 'indoor voices' are to be used inside. Do you see Rule #4 on our chart? It says, 'Use indoor voices in the classroom.' The voice you're using is more appropriate for outdoor play."

Here is a sample set of classroom rules:

1. Listen to the teacher.
2. Listen to one another.
3. Follow directions.
4. Use indoor voices in the classroom.
5. Walk in the classroom.
6. Care for your class friends.

Keys to Effective Classroom Management

◆ Make classroom rules as concrete as possible and help children understand them. Telling a four- or five-year-old to "Keep your hands to yourself when we walk down the hall" or "hitting others in the classroom is not allowed" is much more concrete than "control yourself."

◆ Class rules may need to be explained repeatedly until children grasp the concepts.

Explaining Why Rules Are Necessary

The Issue

Young children need explanations about why rules are part of classroom living. Helping children realize that everyone has a responsibility to develop a "happy classroom" is an essential component of effective classroom management.

Overview

Young children need to understand that there are rules of democratic living and why these rules are essential.

Goal

♦ To help children understand classroom rules and the reasons why these rules exist

Solutions

Important democratic principles young children must learn are:

♦ My wants and needs are not the only ones that must be met.

♦ When I am with others, I need to take turns and share.

♦ Sometimes I have to wait for things to happen.

Once these principles are established and practiced, children can learn about assertiveness and negotiation.

Classroom examples of teachers explaining rules:

♦ "Josh, I know you love playing in the Block Center, but four children are here already. I can help you find another center to play in until someone leaves the block area."

♦ "Deb, when you push to get into line, there's a chance someone will fall. Going to the end of the line is a safer practice."

♦ "Oh, my, I noticed you're marking on Curt's picture. I can certainly understand why Curt objects! Use your own paper instead."

♦ "Mrs. Bolin and I have been talking about the problems our two classes are having at the water fountain when we're on the playground. She and I have agreed that our class will use the water fountain first before we come back to the classroom."

Keys to Effective Classroom Management

♦ Explaining why rules are essential is part of classroom instruction that helps children begin more adult-like thinking. Explaining classroom rules helps children become less egocentric, and in time, helps them recognize how laws are formed in city, state, and national arenas.

Being Consistent With Rules

The Issue

Children notice when you are inconsistent about following through on rules and expectations. Classroom rules require fair, equitable follow-through with each child in the class.

Overview

All children test the limits of rules and if they discover that you do not mean what you say, their negative behavior escalates. Children's willingness and ability to learn independence requires that you be vigilant in your relationships with them.

Goal

◆ To help children establish inner control by maintaining rules consistently

Solutions

Early in the school year, Bill learned that he would receive the special privilege of being sent home when he complained to his teacher about headaches or other perceived ailments. After being sent home three days in a row, his mother sent a note to the teacher indicating that Bill was not sick and that he should be kept at school.

Bill continued his practice of complaints, so his teacher sent him to the nurse for care instead of sending him home. But the nurse determined that, indeed, Bill was not sick, and she discussed the problem with Bill's teacher.

When the teacher had a private conversation with Bill about his made-up illnesses, she told him that she expected him to stay in the classroom and participate in class activities with his classmates. His complaints stopped, and with patience on the part of his teacher, he had a successful kindergarten year.

Keys to Effective Classroom Management

◆ Apply rules consistently for all children.
◆ Sometimes rules should be suspended for out-of-the-ordinary circumstances. For example, children are not allowed to go to another side of the playground except when a special parade comes by. If rules are suspended on special occasions such as this, review the rules when children are again expected to conform to classroom or playground limitations.

Consequences of Behavior

The Issue

No matter the infraction, children need to know that inappropriate behavior has consequences. New teachers occasionally fall into the habit of telling children that something will happen if they continue to behave the way they do, and then no consequence materializes. Consequences help children understand the need for self-control.

Overview

Children who do not follow the rules need to experience some type of consequence. Otherwise, rules have no meaning to them.

Goal

- To help children learn to be independent and to care for themselves and their property, traits that begin in the early years. Consequences give children the sense that what they do has repercussions in everyday life.

Solutions

Note the appropriate consequences in each of the following circumstances:

- The teacher removes Tanisha from the Home Living Center because she continues to hit other children. She talks to Tanisha about her hitting, and then allows her to choose another center.
- Dwight appears to be listening to the story his teacher is reading, but he continues to poke and distract the children sitting around him. His teacher calls his name several times to redirect his attention to the book, but Dwight keeps poking his friends. The teacher finally motions for Dwight to come sit next to her while she continues to read. Dwight's behavior improves.
- Jerome accidentally tore a page in his library book. His teacher requires him to repair the page before returning the book to the library.
- Zach throws one of the classroom balls over the playground fence, and a car hits it and deflates it. Zach's teacher talks to him about the consequences of his behavior and allows the deflated ball to be a sufficient lesson for the incident. No one is able to play with the damaged ball.
- Trisha bit one of her friends while they were playing at the water table. After attending to the child whom Trisha bit, her teacher talks to Trisha about how her biting hurts her friend, telling her that she cannot play at the water table for the rest of the day. The teacher sends a note about the incident to Trisha's parents and to the parents of the child who was bitten. When Trisha returns to the water table the next week, she bites one of her friends again. This time, the teacher talks to Trisha more sternly and removes her again for the rest of the day. She also sends another note home to Trisha's parents about the incident. She requests a conference with Trisha's parents.

Keys to Effective Classroom Management

- Children need explanations about the consequences of their behaviors. Some children have not yet realized that behaviors have consequences. Address negative behaviors and suggest acceptable and positive alternatives.

Complimenting "Good" Behavior

The Issue

Children need to be recognized when they exhibit positive behaviors. Parents and teachers alike support their own values when they observe and compliment the types of behavior they want children to demonstrate. Teachers need to look for the behaviors they want in the classroom and support children's efforts when they see young children demonstrating these behaviors.

Overview

At the beginning of the school year, praise helps communicate to children what behaviors are expected in the classroom. Eventually, children become self-regulated and do not need an abundance of praise to manage themselves.

Goal

◆ To help children feel more secure by letting them know their limitations and the parameters of the classroom setting. Taking time to compliment children's positive behaviors will communicate classroom values and expectations.

Solutions

Examples of complimenting "good" behavior include:

◆ Hajim puts his arm around his friend, Kayli, when she begins to cry. Mrs. Sower compliments him by saying, "You're comforting your friend. Good for you. I'm sure she is feeling better already."

◆ Marshall raises his hand before speaking in Circle Time, a practice that he does not usually demonstrate. His teacher comments, "Good, Marshall, I see you remembered to raise your hand."

◆ Mrs. Martin leans over and whispers into Carrie's ear, "Carrie, you walked down the hall so quietly after we left the gym." Carrie grins widely in response to her teacher's praise.

◆ Mrs. Doyle holds up the class's favorite puppet and asks, "Do you know what Mrs. McGillicutty told me about you today? She said that you were the best kindergarten class that she has ever seen, especially when you walked to the cafeteria. What do you think about that?"

Keys to Effective Classroom Management

◆ An unfortunate fact about the use of praise is that children who do not receive it begin to say, "Look at me, teacher, I'm quiet now. See me! I'm quiet." To avoid conflicts among children and hurt feelings, praise must be used judiciously and always genuinely.

Helping Children Understand Accidental Situations

The Issue

Marissa began to cry when she noticed that she had dropped ketchup on her dress during lunchtime. She seemed inconsolable as her teacher approached her to comfort her.

Overview

The way children learn to respond to upsetting situations will determine how they respond to the disappointments they will experience throughout their lifetimes. Occasionally, children feel overwhelming loss and sadness when events appear to be out of control. Helping children understand and deal with real life (and all its ups and downs) eases their distress and assists them in acquiring coping skills that will be helpful in later life.

Goal

◆ To give children the sympathy and comfort they need when faced with disappointments, but also to help them form a positive attitude toward life. Children cannot (and should not) be sheltered from pain and loss.

Solutions

Marissa's teacher sat down beside her and pulled her close. "Oh, my, Marissa, you're certainly upset about something. Talk to me about it." Once the teacher understood the problem, she explained that the dress would be like new once it was washed and suggested that the two of them find some cold water to wash away the stain. Later, she told Marissa that no one could ever tell that ketchup had been spilled on her dress.

You need to help children manage their emotions. Obviously, Marissa placed high priority on keeping clothes clean, but she also needed to learn that keeping clothes clean forever is impossible. Often, remedies exist for problems, but in other situations, children may have to live with the results. Disappointments that children need assistance with include:

◆ Broken toys or personal items
◆ Messy papers or lost books
◆ Lost clothing
◆ Missing pets
◆ Death of a classroom pet
◆ Death of a classmate
◆ Death of a family member
◆ Broken promises from friends or parents
◆ Missing the bus or arriving late to the classroom

Keys to Effective Classroom Management

◆ When children have more difficulty than usual dealing a difficult life event, such as the death of a pet, suggesting professional assistance beyond the classroom may be necessary.

Using Cueing Signals

The Issue

Mrs. Frezia walked to the light switch in her classroom and flicked the light three times. The children stopped their activities and waited for her directions. This signal is one of several she had demonstrated to the children early in the school year as a means for getting their attention for important announcements.

Overview

Formulate a set of signals to cue children for classroom announcements, routines, or a brief discussion about a classroom issue that needs to be addressed. Some teachers even use private signals for individual children as reminders of behaviors they need to remember.

Goal

◆ To develop cueing signals to gain the children's attention. They are also useful when you need to catch the eye of one child who needs a quiet reminder about his or her behavior.

Solutions

To use cueing systems effectively, make sure children know when and why they will be used. During the first weeks of school, explain the system and practice it with the children. Cueing systems are useful when children become too noisy or seem to be avoiding tasks that are expected of them. Their use is also important when it is time to change activities or move to another component of the daily schedule.

Flicking the classroom lights is one of several commonly used signals. Others include:

- ◆ ringing a bell in the classroom
- ◆ clapping one's hands several times
- ◆ singing a song (see page 47 in Singing Songs for more information)
- ◆ standing in front of the classroom and holding up your hand until everyone's attention is on you
- ◆ using a specific fingerplay (see page 49 in the Doing Fingerplays section for more information)
- ◆ reciting a chant that children can repeat, such as, "If you can hear my voice, clap three times. If you can hear my voice, clap once"
- ◆ motioning children to look at your eyes
- ◆ walking around the classroom and lightly tapping children on their shoulders until all children have turned their attention to you

Keys to Effective Classroom Management

- ◆ Overusing cueing signals can cause the children to think of them as too routine and mundane. Use them when it is necessary to give children gentle reminders about appropriate classroom behavior or for important announcements.

Using the "Remember When" Technique

The Issue

Knox grabbed the sock puppet from Tom's hand and ran around the room whooping and making loud noises. Tom's shocked reaction was to scream loudly at Knox, "That's mine, I was playing with it first!"

Overview

A critical component in the emotional development of young children is their ability to understand the emotions of other children. The "remember when" technique allows children to comprehend another child's emotions by remembering their own in a similar circumstance.

Goal

◆ To teach children about others' viewpoints. Repeated social interactions with you and in groups of children will help them recognize that everyone has similar emotions.

Solutions

Mrs. Cruz had dealt with this type of problem in previous situations, so she moved calmly into Knox's path, bent down to his eye level and said, "Knox, remember last week when Merrilee took the puzzle you were putting together? How did you react?"

Knox presented a sheepish response, "I yelled at her."

"Like Tom is yelling at you now?"

"Yes," and Knox's head bowed lower.

Mrs. Cruz simply asked Knox to put himself into Tom's situation. Once Knox "remembered when" a similar incident occurred to him, he was able to more clearly understand Tom's feelings. With further discussion, Mrs. Cruz persuaded Knox to return Tom's puppet until he was through playing with it. Later, she noticed they were playing together in the Puppet Center, each with a different puppet.

Keys to Effective Classroom Management

◆ Sometimes broader application of this technique is helpful. Understanding the emotions of children in another country might be necessary if youngsters come to school asking about a disaster they have seen on a television news program. "Remember how sad we were when our class hamster died? The people in Mexico City are sad, too, because of the earthquake that killed so many of their friends and family members. Do you think there might be a way we could help them with their problem?"

Diverting Children's Attention

The Issue

Young children are easily distracted by activities that are going on around them. They will fidget and turn to their friends during Circle Time, and they will rush to the window if some event is happening outdoors.

Overview

Recognize that children have many interests. Their inattention is characteristic of their age, and you need to be able to draw them back into discussions and classroom activities.

Goal

◆ To develop strategies to help children focus their attention on group activities

Solutions

To keep children's attention you will need a variety of strategies for drawing children's attention back to the learning at hand. The following are suggestions for diverting children's attention during group time:

◆ Ask the child a question.

◆ Make eye contact with the child and use a nonverbal cue to regain his or her attention.

◆ Call the child's name and tell her you need her attention

◆ Move closer to the child.

◆ Move to the child and put your hand on her shoulder.

◆ Stop what you are doing and wait until the child turns around to see what you're doing.

◆ Ask the child to come sit by you while you continue the discussion, book reading experience, or other activity.

◆ Call the child aside and give her a choice to remain in the group or go to another area of the room (the choice should be a quiet area of the classroom).

◆ As soon as possible after group time, talk to the child about why her behavior is distracting to others.

◆ If children are distracted by a toy or other object another child is holding in his hand, ask the child to put the toy in his cubby or pocket until a later time.

Keys to Effective Classroom Management

◆ Plan short group experiences. Do not expect young children to sit for longer than 15 to 20 minutes.

◆ Sometimes the distracting event may be a more important learning event for the children than the planned experience. Recognize that, on occasion, going with the children's interests may be more important for them. For example, if a plumber walks into the classroom to fix a leaky faucet, the children will learn more by watching him work than continuing the planned activity or experience.

Using Private Time

The Issue

People of all ages need time away from others. If they don't have it, sometimes they become irritable and grouchy in their relationships with others.

Overview

Quiet spaces in the classroom and/or naptime or rest time give preschoolers the opportunity to rest, both physically and emotionally. Children should also learn when it is appropriate to find some quiet time for themselves.

Goal

◆ To help children discover their need for private time and to have spaces in the classroom available to them, which develops their self-control and independence

Solutions

Some of the quiet areas in preschool classrooms are:

◆ a Book Corner
◆ a pile of soft pillows in a quiet corner of the classroom
◆ an old bathtub filled with pillows
◆ a tent with sleeping bags, cots, or mats
◆ a specially prepared loft (perhaps doubling as a Book Nook)
◆ a cot or sofa (if space is available)

Occasionally, you might ask children to move to a "time out" area for a few minutes. This technique must be used with explanation and only for short periods of time. These "time out" chairs, sometimes called "power chairs," are most effective when used positively. Using the "time out" chair for children to regain self-control changes the focus of the chair to one of children learning independence, never as punishment.

Demonstrate the use of the "time out" chair, especially when you are feeling frustrated with the children. The children will notice if you are sitting in "time out." This is a "teachable moment" to explain that you are upset, and that you need to regain your self-control.

Keys to Effective Classroom Management

◆ Private time is important to all individuals and should never be utilized as a punitive control.

Using Indoor and Outdoor Voices

The Issue

Most children love to talk, and the more excited they are, the louder they will talk. If children have limited experiences with groups, they will talk with voices that may be too loud in the classroom environment.

Overview

Youngsters need feedback about the difference between quiet voices used inside and louder voices that are appropriate outdoors.

Goal

◆ To help children use an appropriate voice level when they are inside the classroom. Exceptions may occur when children are highly excited about something they want to tell.

Solutions

When planning classroom rules, talk about the difference between indoor and outdoor voices. Tell the children that when they are indoors, they need to be quieter. When they are outside, they can be louder if they want. The best plan is to demonstrate a quiet voice to children and let them rehearse using quiet voices.

After a few days of reminders, you may discover that children have not recognized the difference between the two. You may need to demonstrate which voice is an indoor voice and which is an outdoors voice. This practice should be a last resort, because negative models are questionable.

Occasionally, children may suggest that they should never talk in the classroom. Let them know that this is an unrealistic expectation, but that quieter voices are necessary within the classroom.

Keys to Effective Classroom Management

◆ Until children internalize their understanding of "indoor" and "outdoor" voices, you will need to provide reminders about the difference.

Singing Songs

The Issue

There may be times, such as rainy days, when children become increasingly rowdy. Even after using a number of cueing signals to remind the children that their voices are becoming too loud, the children quickly become louder than they had been previously. While you are tolerant of the noise in this circumstance, you recognize that the class is disturbing other groups of children. What do you do next?

Overview

Discussing the noise level in the classroom may eliminate children's rowdiness and assist them in remembering classroom rules.

Goal

◆ To help children realize that their noisy behavior may be a problem for others. Children need to be refocused to limit the disruptive behaviors that are emerging.

Solutions

Begin singing a song that all the children know, especially one that brings the children into a circle for a musical game. "Hokey Pokey," "London Bridge Is Falling Down," or "Looby Loo" are good choices, but any well-known tune will accomplish the same results. Choose a song children often request.

Keys to Effective Classroom Management

◆ As a last resort, take the children to the gym or to a covered walkway and let them run. Unfortunately, rainy days seem to make children more active than they usually are.

◆ If you do not feel comfortable singing with the children, a chant, musical recording, or CD will work just as well.

Doing Fingerplays

The Issue

Every group of children will exhibit loud and noisy behavior occasionally. A routine activity, such as a favorite fingerplay, is an effective tool to drawing children to attentive behavior. When the children are quieter, remind them that their voices are too loud and ask them to resume their activities with more self-control.

Overview

Doing group chants with a favorite fingerplay or poem will help the children focus their attention on you and their negative behavior will be diverted. Then talk quietly to them about how they need to be behaving in the classroom, thus providing a quiet and self-restrained model.

Goal

◆ To help children slow their disruptive behavior long enough to join into the recitation. When it's finished, share whatever reminder is needed (much like Cueing Signals described previously on page 42).

Solutions

Choose a favorite fingerplay or poem, so children are more likely to chime in. Try "Five Little Monkeys" or "One, Two, Three, Four, Five"—whatever chant children have requested many times.

Five Little Monkeys
Five little monkeys jumping on the bed
One fell off and bumped his head.
Mama called the doctor, and the doctor said,
"No more monkeys jumping on the bed!"

Repeat, subtracting a monkey each time. Use fingers to act out the rhyme.

One, Two, Three, Four, Five
One, two, three, four, five,
Once I caught a fish alive.
Six, seven, eight, nine, ten,
Then I let it go again.
Why did you let it go?
Because it bit my finger so.
Which finger did it bite?
The little one upon the right.

Keys to Effective Classroom Management

◆ If children do not respond, plan a discussion about group behaviors, including how you expect the children to behave in the classroom.

Playing Games

The Issue

Moving from center activities back to group time requires finesse and expertise, especially when children are noisy and fidgety. Forming a circle for a group game helps children get back into the routine of the day.

Overview

Cueing signals can become mundane when used frequently. Forming a circle and beginning a game that children enjoy eases the transition from play to more formal activity.

Goal

◆ To use songs, fingerplays, and games to bring children's attention back to the routine of the day and to group experiences.

Solutions

Children delight in playing circle games. Try these tips for organizing a game circle:

◆ Chant this rhyme over and again:

Who will ride the bus with me? I will, I will.
Who will ride the bus with me? I will, I will.
Who will ride the bus with me? I will, I will.
Who will ride the bus with me? I will!

Move around the room and motion children to step in behind you, eventually forming a circle in the main area of the classroom. Now it's time to introduce a new game.

◆ Make up a song that children recognize as a signal to form a circle in the classroom. Use a well-known tune as the foundation. Try the following words to "London Bridge Is Falling Down" as an example:

Who can make a circle now, circle now, circle now?
Who can make a circle now? Let's play a game.

◆ While standing in line at the door, try a game of "I Spy." Examples include:
  ◆ "I spy something on the wall that goes 'tick, tock, tick, tock.' What is it?"
  ◆ "I spy a picture of an animal that has four legs, is furry, and says, 'woof, woof.' What is it?"
  ◆ "I spy something that is red, white, and blue. It's a symbol for our country. What is it?"

Keys to Effective Classroom Management

◆ Most strategies become boring if used too often. Vary techniques and approaches to keep children interested in classroom activities.

Putting It Into Practice: Eddie

The principles supporting this narrative are:

- Classroom management requires teachers to deal with individual problems.
- When one technique fails, try another.
- Some children respond quickly, while others require a longer time to respond.
- Involve the family as much as possible when dealing with a child's problems.
- Sharing personal experiences will facilitate children's understanding of their own problems.
- Children may need instruction about expressing their feelings before they can verbalize their needs and concerns.
- Professional assistance beyond the classroom is necessary on occasion.
- Patience and good humor are essential to success.

Ms. Sheldon ran down the hall as fast as she could for the third time this week to catch Eddie. From the very first day of school Eddie seemed unhappy; and in the third week, he began trying to escape from the classroom almost any time the class left the room. Ms. Sheldon remembered that Eddie's mother mentioned that this year in kindergarten was Eddie's first away from home. Eddie's mother worked part time, and during the day, he stayed with an aunt who lived near their home. His older brother was in sixth grade, and the two rarely interacted with one another. Eddie was essentially an only child.

Children who try to escape from school are avoiding classroom activities for a number of reasons:

- They are unaccustomed to long periods of time away from their normal routine.
- They are unaccustomed to being with other children.
- Their teachers have unrealistic expectations for their developmental ages.
- Their parents have not prepared children for school and the responsibilities that are required of them.
- Emotionally, they are not prepared for the schedules and routines of being in school.
- They have emotional problems that prevent them from being happy in a school setting.

Mrs. Sheldon prevented Eddie from running out the school door, gently pulling him close and telling him that his mother expected him to stay at school. He did not resist, but his inactive attention and participation in the remaining activities of the school day told Mrs. Sheldon that she would need to work much harder with Eddie to help him find his niche at school.

In the telephone conversation she had with Eddie's mother that evening, both women agreed that an appropriate plan of action would require both of them to work with Eddie. They needed to determine the source of his unhappiness and develop strategies that would encourage his understanding of the need to stay in school and learn.

(continued on the next page)

Mrs. Sheldon recognized that her early year rigidity and enforcement of rules might be a deterrent to Eddie's happily accepting school as a good place to be. She reminded herself to be more nurturing toward Eddie, and she began the next morning by greeting him warmly and saying, "Eddie, I'm so glad you're in my class. Let's work together so that you can get to know the other children in this classroom and enjoy school. Tell me what you like to do at home."

Mrs. Sheldon called Eddie's mother every week during the first two months of school. She began noticing some subtle differences in Eddie, and it appeared he was developing a close friendship with Jeremy and Sammy. By December, Mrs. Sheldon was not worrying at all about Eddie attempting to run away. He had made himself at home.

Environmental Issues

Chapter 3

When groups of people attend an event such as a rock concert or a championship playoff game, they expect a crowded hall or stadium and noisy participants. The raucous nature of the crowd sometimes erupts into screaming fans, accompanied by jeers or cheers and bellowing responses to the activity on stage or on the field. On rare occasions, fights break out and police control is necessary to bring order back to the event.

Just as the environment has an impact on people in these two situations, the classroom environment influences children. If a room is messy and disorderly, children will become messy and disorderly. If a classroom is warm and inviting and welcomes children to come in and learn, then children will respond accordingly. This chapter shows how teachers can set up classrooms that nurture children and stimulate their intellectual development.

Setting Up an Interesting and Attractive Classroom

The Issue

Young children respond to interesting and attractive classroom environments, and the environment affects how children behave.

Overview

Children need a classroom that has a variety of activities that interest them. Materials should stimulate their thinking, encourage positive social behavior, and be safe for all children to play with. The classroom needs a variety of materials without being overwhelming to young children.

Goal

◆ To set up an interesting, neat, and attractive classroom that will yield positive behaviors from children

Solutions

Suggestions for setting up an interesting and attractive classroom environment include:

◆ Place an inviting sign or poster on the classroom door that suggests that children will enjoy being here (include the name of the teacher or the grade level—Welcome to Mrs. Galloway's Kindergarten Class).
◆ Change bulletin boards periodically to enhance classroom learning.
◆ Display children's work (art is best) whenever possible; consider setting aside one bulletin board that will always have children's work on it.
◆ Personalize the classroom as much as possible (for example, display children's birthdays on a bulletin board).
◆ Display children's names on cubbies, name charts, or bulletin boards (some teachers alphabetize the children's names)

- Provide a message board to write messages to various children during the week.
- Display a Responsibility Board so children will know their duties for the day or week.
- Set up centers that are inviting for children to want use.
- Mark areas of the classroom with attractive signs; designate the desired number of children for each center.
- Create an open area for group activities.
- Provide classroom spaces that offer children privacy when they need it.
- Provide for a variety of sensory experiences for children (water or sand tables, for example, or a textures table).

- Think about traffic flow in the classroom, such as whether the traffic will be disruptive to people in the Book Corner.

Note: The number one factor in organizing the classroom is safety. If any equipment, materials, toys, or games in the classroom are unsafe, remove them immediately.

Keys to Effective Classroom Management

- When children appear bored or listless, wandering aimlessly in the classroom, the time may be right to add a few new toys or introduce a new game to the children.
- Some children respond negatively to bright colors, especially children with special needs. If the classroom is too colorful and busy, tone down the color scheme to prevent children from being distracted by classroom brightness.

Displaying Classroom Rules

The Issue

Developing a set of classroom rules is discussed on page 36 in the previous chapter. Posting the chart in the classroom after it is developed helps everyone remember the rules that were agreed upon.

Overview

Referring to a classroom rules chart when negative behavior occurs is a good classroom management technique. You can remind a child that the rules were agreed upon to help the classroom operate smoothly. If the children helped to develop the rules, you can also remind the child that everyone participated in creating the rule.

Goal

◆ To maintain a safe and orderly classroom environment. Most children will respond to classroom rules, and the result is a group of children who behave appropriately.

Solutions

Establishing classroom rules at the beginning of the school year is a typical procedure in classrooms (see page 36). Periodically throughout the school year, you may need to review the rules to help children remember them. Add a visual component to each of the rules you display, such as a picture of children walking, or other examples of the behaviors you are trying to encourage.

Keys to Effective Classroom Management

◆ Recognize that many events in everyday life, including classroom celebrations, cause children to be less well behaved. With patience and understanding (and reminders about the rules), children will respond.

◆ If children behave inappropriately more than usual on a specific day, sit down with the entire group and review the classroom rules. You might even suggest that a rule be changed if it isn't working well.

Conducting Successful Circle Times

The Issue

Children are expected to participate in group experiences at some point during the school day. For Circle Time or group time to be successful learning experiences for children, plan carefully for their implementation.

Overview

Circle Time is important for developing social skills and provides a foundation for group activities that children are expected to participate in when they enter elementary school. Most children younger than three need small-group experiences (perhaps with a book or a game they can play). For three-year-olds, plan a Circle Time of about 10 minutes. Fours and fives can sit for 15 to 20 minutes. Gradually increase the time as children get older and/or their needs and skills develop.

Goal

♦ To plan the length of Circle Time to match the needs and skills of the children

Solutions

Steps for calling children together for Circle Time and conducting it successfully are:

1. Develop a cueing signal that calls children together for Circle Time (play or sing a predetermined song).

2. As soon as children begin to gather, start a familiar activity (a fingerplay or song that children know).

3. Plan to share the content information at the beginning (children may tire quickly, so present the main focus right away). Address the interests of the children in the group.

4. Allow for group discussion as much as possible; children remember their contributions to discussions and learn from them.

5. Plan for a movement experience to address children's need to move and to prevent them from becoming too fidgety.

6. If it appears that the Circle Time is not working, move on to the next part of the daily schedule (most information is not so important that it cannot be discussed another day).

Keys to Effective Classroom Management

♦ Focus Circle Time on the interests of the children. Like all learning in the classroom, concrete experiences provide first-hand learning for children. Talking about growing wheat in Kansas or cotton farming in Georgia will not be meaningful to children. Bringing in a stem of wheat or a cotton plant that children can experience first-hand will help children learn because the information is concrete.

Planning for Mealtimes

The Issue

Whether lunch and snack times are served in the classroom or another part of the school, mealtime is a hectic time for early childhood educators. Having additional employees or parent volunteers at these times of the day eases the stress and strain on you and the children. However, if neither is available, there are still many things you can do to facilitate an enjoyable mealtime.

Overview

Serving food to children requires planning, just as any other activity during the day. Children do not sit patiently and wait for their food.

Goal

◆ To make meal times orderly and pleasurable

Solutions

Working to achieve the best possible lunch experience for children will have multiple health and social benefits for youngsters. These rules will encourage orderly and fun mealtimes, even if you do not have extra hands to help.

◆ Plan a set time for lunch and snack.
◆ Let parents know when lunch is scheduled, so they can plan accordingly. When possible, invite parents to join their children for lunch.
◆ Make sure that children wash their hands prior to eating (monitor, if necessary).
◆ Ensure that the tables are cleaned before children eat and after they finish.
◆ At least one adult should sit down and eat with the children. Family style meals are better, if they can be planned and implemented.
◆ Model social behaviors expected when meals are served.
◆ Encourage children to have social discussions during lunch.
◆ Meals should be leisurely and enjoyable, never rushed.
◆ Instruct children about cleaning up after their meals (for example, remove trays and trash and dispose of them appropriately).

Keys to Effective Classroom Management

◆ Periodically reflect on mealtime experiences to determine whether they are meeting your educational goals for children. If necessary, change the way lunch is served. Do not continue a chaotic mealtime experience and do not continue the way lunch is served if children are not learning from it.

Providing Choices

The Issue

A typical preschool daily schedule provides long periods of time when children must choose activities they want to participate in. Establishing a system for children to make choices fosters independence and decision-making skills.

Overview

Children need to know their range of choices; but they also need to know that once a choice is made, they must maintain their activity until it is time to transition to a new activity.

Goal

◆ To help children learn to make choices

Solutions

During the first week of school, introduce the different centers in your classroom, and then let children choose where they want to play. Usually center time is 45 to 60 minutes in length. Explain to the children that, once they have decided where they wish to play, they must remain there until center time is over. Guidelines to facilitate effective center time experiences include:

◆ Limit the number of children in each center, probably no more than five children for most centers.

◆ Tell children they must stay in the center they choose.

◆ If children are behaving inappropriately in a center, remove them for a short time and talk to them about more appropriate behaviors.

◆ If children behave inappropriately when they return to their chosen center, remove them a second time and ask them to make another choice.

◆ If there are numerous centers in the classroom, provide an option for children to choose a second center (providing the numbers of children in the center allow for them to move).

◆ Periodically close a center to encourage choices that are being overlooked.

◆ Play in one of the classroom centers, because when you spend time in a particular center it encourages children to join in the play.

Keys to Effective Classroom Management

◆ A child may have little or no experience making choices. When first providing choices, limit the number of choices so the decision-making is less overwhelming. Initially, give the child two choices, then three. Once the child has confidence in making decisions, then it will become easier to choose from several options.

Thinking About the Environment

The Issue

When arranging classroom environments, consider what the space invites children to do. Does it invite children to make choices? Will the space be attractive and encourage learning? Will the space suggest to children that they run and behave as if they were outdoors? Does the space curtail boisterous behavior? Does its design promote self-management and democratic living?

Overview

The environmental design of a classroom has an impact on how children learn and behave. Smaller, more comfortable areas persuade children to play, thus promoting interpersonal interactions, dramatic representations, and vocabulary development.

Goal

◆ To create a well-organized classroom that will support positive classroom behavior

Solutions

Look at the classroom space, and ask these questions:

◆ Is the space divided into areas of learning that are easily determined?
◆ Are the play spaces small enough to provide children with intimate interactions?
◆ Does the classroom setup prohibit children from running?
◆ Can you easily see all children when you observe the space?
◆ Are enough materials available for all children to participate?
◆ Can individuals easily move around the classroom?

Keys to Effective Classroom Management

◆ If a classroom space needs to be rearranged, children can help with moving furniture, equipment, and supplies.

Planning for Transitions

The Issue

A "transition" is a time during the schedule when children move from one activity to another. Usually transitions are associated with changes groups of children make during the day. Examples of transitions are arrival to school; dismissal; going outdoors; lining up to go to another part of the school or center; moving to classroom centers; returning to group activities; moving to Circle Time; and so on. Often, transitions are difficult for young children.

Overview

Planning for transitions helps children move from one activity to another much more easily.

Goal

◆ To help children begin to understand how to transition from one activity to the next

Solutions

Plan for transitional changes, so children can make them with little disruption or rowdiness. Here are some suggestions for making transitions:

◆ Use a cueing signal to announce the transitional change (see page 42 for more information about signals to consider).

◆ Ask children to move in a specific way (tiptoe, crawl, pretend to skate, pretend to be a caterpillar, walk like a cat, twinkle like a star, or others).

◆ Call children to line up by the color of their clothing. ("Everyone wearing blue can line up at the door; now everyone wearing red," and so on.)

◆ Call children to Circle Time (or the next activity of the day) by the color of their eyes or hair.

◆ Observe children as they clean up, and as they finish, tell them it's their turn to line up at the door (or come to Circle Time or whatever part of the day you are transitioning to).

◆ Ask individual children for information (their address or phone number). If they have trouble with the facts, help them clarify the information they need before sending them to the classroom activity they have selected.

◆ For older children, suggest they move according to the letter in their first name. ("All children whose names begin with 'P' can go wash their hands.")

◆ Begin by tapping one child who, in turn, taps another, who taps another, until all the children have been tapped to move.

◆ Ask the line leader to decide what transition to use.

◆ Ask one child to name a favorite song, which becomes the tune to move by.

Keys to Effective Classroom Management

◆ All learning in the classroom requires instruction. Creating smooth transitions means the teacher has to plan for them and teach children why it is important to use them.

Organizing Centers

The Issue

Children enjoy center time, but placing children in centers takes planning, allowing for choices and for changes (if available as an option).

Overview

Until children become familiar with the center time experience, there may be some confusion and chaos. Talking to individual children about their choices and reminding them that they need to stay in their chosen center for the duration of the scheduled time (or when they can change centers, if that is possible) will help smooth out problems.

Goal

◆ To create center-time experiences that offer choices and productive play experiences

Solutions

Use a "Center Time Board" to give children opportunities to make choices or change choices. Post indicators about how many children can be in a center. These indicators might include:

◆ envelopes with numbers or symbols on them, which children put their name tags in.

◆ map tacks placed under a picture of the center labeled with a number or symbol (children place the tack underneath a desired center).

◆ pegs placed under a picture of the center labeled with a number or symbol (again, children place the peg underneath a desired center).

A few tips for facilitating center-time choices are:

◆ Limit the number of children who can choose a specific center (post the limit so the children can see it and understand it or use a "Center Time Board" for children to make choices).

◆ Tell children that they must stay in the center they choose for the duration of the play period.

◆ If children behave inappropriately during center time, remove them from the center for a short time and explain to them why they are being removed. Give them a chance to return to their play. If they behave inappropriately again, they will need to choose a second center.

◆ If enough centers are available, plan for children to leave their first center choice and move to another by using a "Center Time Board."

Long periods of time are important for productive and creative play experiences for children. At first, very young children may have difficulty extending their play. Help these children by making suggestions and participating in the play.

Keys to Effective Classroom Management

◆ Children often choose the same center over and over. Although children may want to use the same center again and again, encourage them to choose other centers with one of the following four strategies:
1. closing the popular center occasionally
2. playing in a less popular center periodically (children like to be where the teacher is)
3. talking to children about the merits of less popular centers
4. providing a special activity in one of the less popular centers

Tips for Creating Child-Friendly Centers

Art Center

◆ Place the Art Center near a water source.
◆ Place the Art Center on a floor surface that can be cleaned easily (for example, on tile or linoleum, not carpet).
◆ Determine the number of children who can participate in the Art Center based on the activities available (for example, as many as six children could play with clay or work with markers or crayons).
◆ Limit the number of children who can paint to the number of easels in the classroom.
◆ Put a painter's drop cloth or a vinyl picnic tablecloth under easels.
◆ Provide paint smocks for every child who is painting.
◆ Instruct children about the use of paints and other art materials.
◆ Provide a drying rack for children to use when they finish painting.
◆ Provide a place for children to display their art products.
◆ Encourage children to clean themselves and their work area after they participate in art activities.

Block Center

◆ Limit the number of children in the Block Center to five or six.
◆ If wooden blocks are used, check them periodically to determine if any are damaged. Remove them if they might be harmful to children.

- Establish the rule that no one may destroy another child's block structure.
- Children may build block structures that are only as tall as they are. (If cardboard blocks are used, this rule is not necessary.)
- Remind children about appropriate ways to dismantle their block structures.
- Encourage group participation in building block structures.
- Periodically, take photographs of children's block structures to share with parents or to place on a bulletin board.

Book Corner

- Place the Book Corner in a quiet section of the classroom.
- Limit the number of children in the Book Corner to about four.
- Look at the books occasionally to find out if any need to be repaired.
- Add new books regularly (about every two weeks) to keep children interested. Use books that complement the topics you are exploring in the classroom. Remove books when children appear to be bored by them. Some books will remain more popular than others throughout the year.
- Display books so that their covers show. This helps children remember the books and increases their interest in the books.
- Remove books that are not used very often.
- Consider having a listening station in the Book Corner.
- If pillows are used in the Book Corner, wash them periodically.
- Provide small stuffed animals so that children can read to them.

Writing Center

- Provide paper, pencils, markers, map pencils, stationery, crayons, and an old typewriter to encourage children to experiment with writing.
- Display an alphabet chart in the center for easy access by children.
- Provide envelopes for children who want to mail their "letters" or art creations.
- Use holiday or birthday cards to serve as models for children's writing.
- Have a bulletin board nearby if children choose to display their writing.
- Provide simple books with large print that children might copy if they choose.
- Make available templates for children to trace letters.
- Have a message board available to post notes to children. Your writing will prompt children's attempts to write.

Dramatic Play Center

- Limit the number of children in the Dramatic Play Center to four or five.
- Make sure that the dress-up clothing in the center is clean and in good repair.

- Wash the clothing periodically to ensure cleanliness.
- Encourage children to make props in the Art Center to use in the Dramatic Play Center.
- Make sure that the props cannot be turned into weapons that will hurt others.

Home Living Center

- Limit the number of children in the Home Living Center to four or five.
- Change props occasionally to encourage multicultural play activity.
- Include dolls and toys that represent a variety of cultures.
- Ensure that the props remain clean and do not need repair.
- Add props according to units being studied in the classroom.
- Consider props that will develop literacy. Examples include telephone books, recipe books, magazines, newspapers, and catalogs.
- If props are made of cloth, wash them periodically.
- Place the Home Living Center near the Dramatic Play Center or Special Interests Centers (such as a Grocery Store Center) to encourage extended play experiences.

Manipulatives/Puzzles Center

- Three or four children should be able to play in this center.
- Choose materials that appropriate for the ages of the children in the class. If pieces are small enough for children to choke on, remove them.
- Mark each puzzle piece from one puzzle with the same number (for example, all pieces of the tractor puzzle have the number 12 on them).
- Make sure that puzzles have all of their pieces. If pieces are missing, remove the puzzle.
- Change puzzles and other manipulative materials periodically to ensure adequate challenge for children.

Outdoor Area

- All children should be able to play in the outdoor play area. Consult specific state and local guidelines for space requirements for the children you teach.

- Inspect playground equipment regularly to determine if repairs need to be made.
- Provide grassy areas as well as graveled surfaces to allow for different types of play.
- Traffic flow is as important on the playground as it is indoors.
- Supervise children at all times when they are playing outdoors.
- Erect fences and secure gates around play areas for children from infancy through age eight.
- Plan for only one or two groups of children to be on the playground at a time.
- Occasionally add Frisbees, colored chalk, and bubbles for a change of pace.

Special Centers

- Encourage the development of special centers based on children's interests and planned thematic studies.
- Limit children's participation to approximately three or four individuals.
- If children bring items from home to contribute to the center, examine the items carefully to determine if they are safe.
- Position the center in a busy area of the classroom. Dismantle Special Interest Centers when children's curiosity seems to wane.

Woodworking Center

- This center is more appropriate for older preschoolers.
- Limit the number of children in the Woodworking Center to three or four.
- Provide instruction in using the carpentry tools.
- Include discarded Styrofoam packing from large boxes so children will not get hurt when they try their carpentry skills.
- Have plenty of scrap materials to encourage children's creativity.
- Monitor the Woodworking Center carefully to prevent accidents.

Putting It Into Practice: Derrick

The principles supporting this narrative are:

- Classroom management requires teachers to deal with individual problems.
- When one technique fails, try another.
- Some children respond quickly, while others require a longer time to respond.
- Involve the family as much as possible when dealing with a child's problems.
- Sharing personal experiences will facilitate children's understanding of their own problems.
- Children may need instruction about expressing their feelings before they can verbalize their needs and concerns.
- Professional assistance beyond the classroom is necessary on occasion.
- Patience and good humor are essential to success.

Mrs. Atkins began noticing the children's responses to her classroom environment the moment they arrived at the child care center on the first day of the school year. Her classroom space was not as large as she would have liked, but she managed to develop several interest centers she knew would be popular with four-year-olds: Home Living Center, Blocks, Book Nook, Puzzles and Manipulatives, Art, and a Discovery Table. With only 12 children, these centers would provide enough choices initially to match children's interests, especially if she changed materials in the centers routinely.

Derrick became a concern for Mrs. Atkins early in the year. He seemed like a happy child, and his mother dressed him appropriately for classroom activities. His arrival was prompt each morning, and his mother reported that he was enjoying the preschool experience. But Derrick did not seem to join in with the other children. Although he sat in group time with the other children, he rarely participated in discussion. When he had something to say, he came to Mrs. Atkins at another time to talk to her privately, often displaying knowledge far beyond his years. During Center Time activities, he tended to be an onlooker, rather than a player. He was not a problem child, per se, but Mrs. Atkins wanted to help him become more social in the classroom.

The first strategy she used was to talk to Derrick's mom. She learned that he was the older of two children, the second having been born only a few months prior to Derrick's school entrance. Derrick's mother admitted that Derrick had had few opportunities to be with older children during his first four years. She had spent a great deal of time talking with her son about all kinds of topics, and his range of knowledge was broad. This was Derrick's first classroom experience, and Mrs. Atkins believed his lack of social expertise stemmed from his lack of experiences with other children.

She began talking to Derrick as soon as he came to school each morning, encouraging him to try some of the activity choices where many children were engaged. She would request that one of the more experienced children help Derrick make the transition into their play setting. She also developed a system of pairing children together when they left the classroom for outdoor play or any other school function. Each time, she attempted to pair

(continued on the next page)

Derrick with children who were more socially adept. She also planned group time lessons to talk about how to make friends and the responsibilities everyone has in developing social relationships.

In addition, Mrs. Atkins asked Derrick's mother to provide some social activities away from home for Derrick—asking a classmate to go the park or going for an ice cream cone together. Eventually, Mrs. Atkins was able to observe Derrick becoming friendlier to others in the class and less dependent on her for his friendship. Derrick just needed information about how to socialize and become friends with others his age.

Daily Routines and Schedules

Chapter 4

Daily rituals and schedules have an impact on how children behave and what they learn. Teachers meet the needs of children by giving them time for reflection and self-initiated experiences. Learning just cannot be rushed!

Young children are just beginning their life's journey to knowing who they are, what they want to do with their lives, and what they will contribute to society. Finding their niche in society happens as they live their lives. *All I Ever Really Needed to Know I Learned in Kindergarten* (Fulgham, 1987) is a testimony that the author's teacher understood that quality education and character development is worthy of our dearest endeavors.

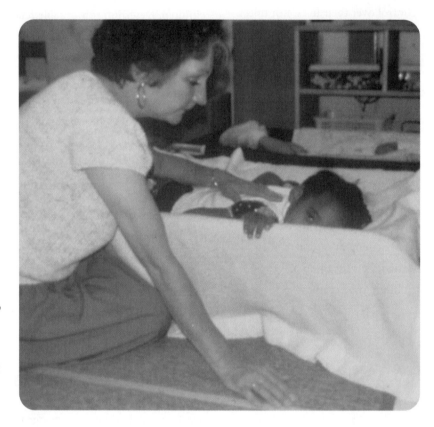

Children Need Routine

The Issue

Routines assist children in their attempts to be self-regulated. When schedules and routines are disrupted, children become grumpy and difficult to live with.

Overview

Keeping children to a flexible, yet stable, routine gives them a sense of control over their lives. Routines cut down on stress, which causes children to become irritable and unreasonable. Disrupted schedules promote disruptive behavior. Talk to any parent during the weeks leading up to a special family celebration or holiday, and their response will indicate how chaotic children's behavior can be when their daily routines are changed. The excitement of out-of-the-ordinary events often causes children to be cranky.

Goal

◆ To establish routines and predictable environments to help children maintain balance, even when guests or special trips demand a schedule change. Unusual events can occur on any day.

Solutions

Beginning activities at a set time, having snacks and lunch at the same time, and going outside at a set time are hallmarks of a good program for young children. Determine a workable schedule, post it in the classroom and school, and follow it as closely as possible every day. Children rely on routines to maintain a happy temperament.

Routines are good for parents to know about, as well. If a doctor's appointment must be scheduled, a parent can work around the child's favorite time of day to keep the disruption to a minimum. For example, if Walker loves to have lunch with the other children in his class, his mother can schedule his doctor visit after lunch to allow Walker social time with his classmates.

Out-of-the-ordinary events, such as a special guest or a monthly visit from a community storyteller, will upset the routine. Plan for these arrivals by talking to children about the change in routine and about when the usual schedule will resume. It is also a good time to talk about how important it is to be polite to guests in the classroom.

Keys to Effective Classroom Management

◆ Prepare children for a change in the schedule.
◆ Talk about what is expected of children when the routine is disrupted.

Children Need Familiar Faces

The Issue

When Deborah arrived one morning, she noticed immediately that her teacher, Ms. Williams, was not there. "Where's my teacher?" she asked. "Ms. Williams is ill this morning," responded the substitute teacher. "I'm Ms. Burris; I'll be your teacher today. Mrs. Williams hopes to be back in the morning."

Overview

Children need familiar people in their classrooms. Deborah, like the other children in her class, seemed out of sorts all day. Ms. Burris followed the lesson plans left for her, and she tended to the children's needs throughout the day. But Ms. Burris was not Ms. Williams, and the children felt a sense of abandonment because their usual teacher was not there. Knowing children's needs and what they need to learn is an easier process when teachers are familiar to children. Both teachers and children will benefit from being with one another for long periods of time.

Goal

◆ To create continuity of care for children by developing a list of substitute teachers to call on when you cannot be in the classroom

Solutions

Most schools and child care centers have a set list of substitutes they call when someone needs to be absent. Substitutes also have training designed to help them understand the needs of young children and the importance of following a posted schedule and lesson plans the teacher has left for them.

Once children become familiar with the same substitutes, they are less apprehensive when the teacher has to be away from school. If you know in advance that you will be absent, you can say, "Ms. Burris will be here again tomorrow, but I plan to be back on Monday. Be sure to help her with the schedule."

Having an adult who children know and feel comfortable with in the classroom is important. In a similar vein, some schools move teachers with the group of children they were assigned initially. This practice is often referred to as "looping" or "primary teaching." After a year or two with the same children, the teacher loops back to a younger group and begins the process again.

Keys to Effective Classroom Management

◆ To the degree possible, prepare children for a new face ahead of time. If children know that a substitue will be teaching for only a day or two, they may be more responsive to the unfamiliar teacher.

Planning for Physical Needs

The Issue

Mrs. Losack planned a Circle Time that had been successful in previous years, and she believed the children would respond positively this year. She had barely begun Circle Time when she noticed that most of the children were fidgeting and moving around. She continued for a while, but she finally realized that she had to stop Circle Time—the children needed something else right now!

Overview

Children need physical activity every day, but some days children need more physical activity than others. Even after being on the playground for the usual amount of time, you are not going to coax children into a listening/sitting activity if they need more time to work out their wiggles! Mrs. Losack made the right decision to change her plans to address children's physical needs.

Goal

◆   To meet children's physical needs so they are more able to participate in planned activities, and more social and emotionally able to interact with other children

Solutions

You can meet children's physical needs in the following ways:

◆   Take children outdoors every day for physical activity.

◆   Provide long blocks of time for indoor play.

◆   Include brief physical breaks during group times.

◆   Develop movement experiences appropriate for children's age.

◆   Utilize music activities that also include physical movements.

◆   Limit the amount of fine motor activity children are required to do.

◆   Allow children to make suggestions about physical activities.

Keys to Effective Classroom Management

◆   In addition to the need to move, children's physical needs also include having enough water and nutritious food to maintain good health.

Planning for Social Needs

The Issue

The social interactions that children have are as important as any learning that goes on in classrooms.

Overview

Jimmy Hymes, an early childhood educator, said, "The best toy for a two-year-old is another two-year-old." Children learn from one another when they socialize, and learning how to be social is as important as intellectual activities. Providing time for socialization and modeling social skills are the two best strategies for helping children acquire the skills they need.

Goal

◆ To expose children to social activities so they can learn social skills effectively

Solutions

How do you plan for social needs? The following are some suggestions:

◆ Provide extended periods of time for play (both indoors and outdoors) when children will naturally interact with one another.

◆ Observe while children are playing to identify children who need help joining play settings (see page 90 for more information).

◆ Model social behaviors for children (formally and informally).

◆ Use group times to talk about social behaviors.

◆ Demonstrate appropriate and inappropriate skills to children with puppets; ask children to tell which demonstration is appropriate and ask why.

◆ Occasionally pair children who have good social skills with children who need more social development to facilitate the social development of the child with weaker skills.

◆ Read children's books that introduce social skills, such as *The Rainbow Fish* by Marcus Pfister and *How to Be a Friend* by Laurie Krasny and Marc Brown.

◆ Demonstrate to children the repercussions of negative social skills (for example, if a child accidentally bumps into the teacher, as an example, she could pretend to cry).

Keys to Effective Classroom Management

◆ Like most learning, social skills require time to learn. Be patient in your expectations of young children's development.

Planning for Emotional Needs

The Issue

Children have difficulty keeping a balanced emotional life. They sometimes cry, fret, whine, throw temper tantrums, and respond emotionally to incidents they experience.

Overview

Children work on managing their emotions for several years. Even older children react emotionally to situations that irritate them or make them feel inferior. Young children will need sympathy, of course, but they also need instruction about handling their emotions. You have a responsibility to assist young children in managing their emotions, especially during the preschool years.

Goal

◆ To help children learn to manage their emotions

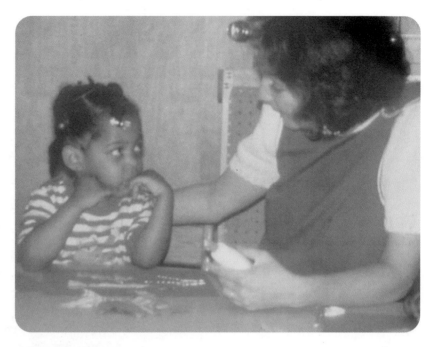

Solutions

When you observe children who are emotionally upset, you have several options for dealing with children's responses:

◆ Talk to the child and determine the source of her emotions.

◆ Tell the child that it's difficult to know why someone is upset and ask him to use his words instead.

◆ If the child is unable to verbalize her problem, try phrasing a possible reason for her tears. ("It looks like you're upset because your doll's dress is torn. Is that right?")

◆ If the problem can be solved, tell the child how the problem might be alleviated.

◆ When the child is calm, explain that everyone experiences reasons for being upset. Then ask the child to talk about her problem, and tell her that talking helps the listener understand what is wrong.

When you observe children managing their emotions, comment positively about their actions.

Keys to Effective Classroom Management

◆ Emotional responses to life's events are to be expected. Be prepared to sympathize with children when they are genuinely upset.

Planning for Intellectual Development

The Issue

Parents expect children to learn when they go to school. Legislators continue to set standards and expectations about what teachers should teach and children should learn. Planning for intellectual development is imperative.

Overview

Because children are naturally curious, they will automatically learn in classrooms. The learning that happens in preschool classrooms helps children begin to acquire the skills and knowledge they will need to become active, productive citizens in their communities.

Goal

- To provide numerous and varied opportunities for children to learn

Solutions

Children learn in many ways. The following are tips for a variety of learning situations:

- Prepare lessons that are short and to the point.
- Set specific objectives for each lesson.
- At a later time, assess children's knowledge to determine if they need more practice or additional information.
- Plan classroom activities that extend learning that has been presented formally (for example, if a lesson was about farm animals, include a set of farm animal photographs in the Manipulatives Center so children can match animals with their babies).
- Plan field trips to expose children to firsthand learning.
- Add toys and equipment to centers that help children learn.
- Observe children as they play in centers to discover what they are learning.
- Individualize learning by sitting with children and asking questions to find out what they know.
- Ask individual children to share knowledge with groups at later times.
- Include books and children's magazines that introduce information to young children.
- Ask parents to come in and interact with children about topics of interest to them.
- Encourage older preschoolers to write or dictate stories or keep journals about what they know.
- Keep checklists and records of children's informal classroom learning.

Keys to Effective Classroom Management

- Daily interactions between teachers and children and among children are a guarantee that children are learning. When children talk with adults, they hear language they may not know, and they internalize knowledge that adults share. When they talk to their peers, the same learning process is occurring. All of us learn from one another when interactions occur.
- Be prepared to answer children's questions and provide information even when you do not know the answer. Respond to a question by saying, "You know, I'm not sure of the answer. Let's look for an answer in our Book Corner."

Planning a Workable Schedule

The Issue

Meeting children's needs includes planning a schedule that provides activities that address the developmental areas of all children.

Overview

Children need quiet time, active time, group time, private time, time for food, and so on. Plan a routine that meets children's physical, social, emotional, intellectual, and creative needs.

Goal

◆ To create predictable, workable schedules that will yield predictable behavior from children

Solutions

Follow these guidelines for developing a workable schedule:

◆ Expect children to sit in groups for only a short period of time (20 minutes is a maximum time frame).

◆ Plan periods of time for children to participate in self-selected activities (an hour is a good length of time).

◆ Remember children's physical, social, emotional, and intellectual needs during the day.

◆ Outdoor play is essential to children's physical development.

◆ The schedule should be predictable (follow the same routine every day).

◆ When the schedule has to be rearranged, try to be calm, patient, and understanding of children's responses to the change.

Keys to Effective Classroom Management

◆ If possible, forewarn children of any expected change in the schedule.

◆ Work together with other teachers and administrators to plan schedules that mesh well with other classrooms. Carefully plan lunch and snack, library, playground, and gym times.

Planning for Emergencies

The Issue

No one likes to believe that emergencies will occur in the classroom or on the playground. But accidents happen, and you need to prepare for unforeseen emergencies.

Overview

If you are alert to potential emergencies, it may be possible to prevent or alleviate them. Scrutinizing the classroom and playground for potential hazards is the first step in planning to reduce accidents.

Goal

- To help everyone know what to do in an emergency so everyone can respond effectively when accidents occur

Solutions

Work with children to avoid emergencies. Here are some tips to follow:

- Eliminate hazards that might cause children to have accidents, such as chairs that are placed in classroom traffic paths.
- Ask children to scrutinize the environment, too, to assist in eliminating dangerous equipment or other safety hazards.
- Invite a safety expert to come in and talk to the children about ways to avoid accidents and mishaps.
- Have a first aid kit available in the classroom.
- Invite the school nurse to talk about her responsibilities when accidents occur.
- Invite emergency personnel to show children how they look when they rescue people. (Firefighters, for example, look quite different when they are wearing their gear.)
- Teach children the "stop, drop, and roll" technique (for fire emergencies).
- Teach children how to dial 911 and what to say if an emergency occurs (at school and at home).
- Have fire drills or tornado drills, so children will know what they need to do in case of an emergency.
- Play a game with children about situations that are emergencies. (Tell the children stories or show them pictures of situations, and then ask them to say whether the emergency is severe enough to call 911.)
- Alert parents to ongoing class discussions about emergencies, so they can talk to their children at home about possible accidents or mishaps.

Keys to Effective Classroom Management

- Some children will become frightened when discussions of emergencies occur in the classroom (perhaps because of prior experiences with fires or accidents). Be sensitive to children's responses, and comfort those who need nurturing during the classroom talk.

Helping Children Develop Perseverance

The Issue

Occasionally, children are unable to conform to the classroom schedules and routines because they are too wiggly or are unable to focus on an activity for an extended period of time. Helping children stay on task is a skill that requires thought and planning.

Overview

When children come to the classroom, expecting them to sit for a long period of time is unreasonable. Young children like to move and explore to find out about the world around them. As they grow older, however, they will need to be able to sit still and listen for directions.

Goal

◆ To learn to first ask children to participate in any classroom activity for just a few minutes at a time, thereby setting the stage for longer periods of participation on subsequent days

Solutions

When it appears that a child is ready to bolt from a "sitting still" time, such as Circle Time or story reading session, try one of these options:

◆ Ask her to stay "just one more minute."
◆ Ask her a question about the story that she should be able to answer.
◆ Ask all the children to stand and shake a minute and then settle down again.
◆ Gently touch the child as a reminder that she needs to sit still just a little bit longer.
◆ Begin singing a song that you know the child enjoys.
◆ Make a gesture or relevant sound that matches the story or Circle Time experience, thus attracting the child's attention.

If a child appears to be having a difficult time choosing a center and instead is wandering around the room from center to center, try one of these techniques:

◆ Take the child by the hand and begin talking to her. Assist the child in choosing a center.
◆ Ask the child to join you in an activity.
◆ Move to a center you know the child likes and start interacting with the children there. Stay there until the unoccupied child joins you (or another center).
◆ Sometimes, pairing a child with a partner helps her become more interested in classroom activities.
◆ Over a period of weeks, monitor the child's time in various centers. Encourage her to stay in centers that she seems to like the most.
◆ Acknowledge children when they stick with a task longer than usual.

Keys to Effective Classroom Management

◆ Children need opportunities to govern their own behaviors. Helping them select activities they enjoy and continue to enjoy these activities is important to children's overall development.

Putting It Into Practice: Andrew

The principles supporting this narrative are:

- Classroom management requires teachers to deal with individual problems.
- When one technique fails, try another.
- Some children respond quickly, while others require a longer time to respond.
- Involve the family as much as possible when dealing with a child's problems.
- Sharing personal experiences will facilitate children's understanding of their own problems.
- Children may need instruction about expressing their feelings before they can verbalize their needs and concerns.
- Professional assistance beyond the classroom is necessary on occasion.
- Patience and good humor are essential to success.

It was early spring and the children were working on the classroom flower project, decorating a mural with a variety of interesting craft materials. Judy Carson, the teacher of the four-year-olds, was quite pleased with the project and the children were intrigued with the new craft materials. Judy looked across from the Art Center and saw Andrew heading for the Block Center again. Regardless of the task or play, Andrew tired of the activity and was ready to move to another project. And, within a short time, he would be ready to move again.

Circle Time was the most difficult time of the day for Andrew, and rarely could he sit on his mat for more than five minutes before running across the room to play with the center toys. Most of the other children had learned to write their names. Andrew was never able to sit still long enough to write and was constantly in motion. It seemed as though Judy spent much of her day trying to direct Andrew to the task at hand. Standing in line was very difficult for Andrew, and he usually had to hold the teacher's hand in line. Judy knew that Andrew was smart and had strong language skills and a keen ability to take things apart. He knew all of the words to every song, and he demonstrated well-developed gross motor skills on the playground. Judy knew that she would need some new strategies for Andrew. Recently, she had attended a workshop on working with children with behavioral difficulties and was ready to put what she had learned into practice.

Judy kept a log of Andrew's problem behaviors throughout the next week. By doing so, she saw that his problem behavior primarily involved getting up from his place and leaving an activity before it was finished. She observed that he was able to stay on task better when there was opportunity for movement or singing. She also learned from her observations of Andrew that the pay-off for leaving an activity was the opportunity to do something else, i.e., another activity.

The first step that Judy decided to take was to pair music and movement with activities that were difficult for Andrew. Rather than singing songs at the beginning and end of Circle Time, Judy spaced songs frequently throughout the time they spent in circle. She noticed that this helped him to stay on task—and it seemed to help several other children stay focused,

(continued on the next page)

as well. Judy also began using more fingerplays and gross motor games during Circle Time. Just when Andrew was beginning to fidget, she reminded him that there would be just one more thing to do, and then they would be finished.

Judy revisited her classroom schedule and made some changes. She alternated active play and more structured activities so that finishing the structured activity provided the child the natural reward of moving to active play when it had been completed.

Judy worked with the class during Circle Time on "listening with your whole body." Each day at the beginning of Circle Time, she reminded the children about listening with their seven body parts. She also acknowledged the fact that they were such good listeners.

In analyzing her classroom space, Judy realized that the centers were easily viewed from the learning circle and the worktable. She recognized that the centers were serious distractions for Andrew. With a minor reconfiguration of the classroom she was able to have more definite boundaries for places for activities. She also removed the temptation of toys by turning the shelves so that the children would not see them from the learning circle.

Judy had spoken with Andrew's mother about her concern for his ability to stay on task at each of the parent conferences. Andrew's mother expressed her opposition to medication, and they both agreed that such a decision was premature. They were both hoping that Andrew would mature during the year, but unfortunately this did not happen during the regular course of the school year. At the spring parent conference, Judy and Andrew's mother brainstormed some times at home when he would be able to work on staying seated and finishing projects. Andrew's mother decided that she would work with him on staying seated to eat his meals; he was in the habit of taking his food to the den and eating it in front of the television when he was tired of sitting. Finally, she talked of her plans to give Andrew some regular responsibilities around the house such as emptying the wastebaskets.

This plan for Andrew was not a "quick fix," nor did it consist of just one simple teacher action. Judy worked with Andrew to teach him new skills, but she also changed her classroom environment and instructional practices. Andrew's mother was supportive and developed a plan to help him with his behavior at home. Although he was not staying on task as long as the other children were at the end of the school year, he did make substantial improvement. Judy knew that with the help of his teachers and parents that Andrew would become a success story!

Building Caring Communities

Chapter 5

Looking around her classroom, Ms. Olsen noted that Hugo was building again in the Block Center. "He loves to build," she thought, "I wonder if he'll grow up to be a carpenter like his dad."

Most teachers experience similar visions of the children in their care as adults, just by watching them in their play and in group activities within the classroom. They see future civic leaders, teachers, politicians, firefighters, diplomats, engineers, and other career possibilities. The early childhood classroom is a microcosm of the community in which they live.

One of the goals of a developmentally appropriate classroom is to develop a caring community. The early years are an excellent time for instilling care and concern for others, helping children understand one another's cultures and viewpoints, and establishing an esprit d'corps among children that will lead to positive interactions. The classroom management techniques outlined in this chapter will help children develop skills that they will need in their later quest for happy adult lives.

Teaching Negotiation Skills

The Issue

Sometimes young children have temper tantrums, grab things, or pout to get what they want. These methods are neither acceptable nor productive. Instead, children need to be taught to negotiate for what they want.

Overview

As children mature to adulthood, they should possess strategies for achieving goals and obtaining things they want. Negotiation skills are essential in most business and educational arenas. Being able to negotiate is a critical skill.

Goal

◆   To help children learn negotiation skills by modeling what to do and by helping children practice negotiation skills

Solutions

Negotiation skills are learned best by modeling adult behavior. The following is an example:

Matthew begins to pout because he cannot play with one of the three classroom tricycles. How can you help? You observe Matthew pouting, go to him, and ask him what the problem is. He tells you that he cannot ride any of the trikes because they are all taken. You confront his pouting behavior by asking if he had considered asking one of the children if he could have a turn. You and Matthew approach the children who are riding trikes to determine if Matthew might have a turn.

Steps for assisting a child with a problem are:

◆   Help the child identify and understand the specific problem he wants to address.

◆   Ask for suggestions for changing the situation. Also, it may be necessary to help him recognize that the problem cannot be solved (see page 89).

◆   Ask the child to determine if a change can be made.

◆   Help him identify and eliminate suggestions that are not feasible.

◆   Follow through on the option the child has chosen.

This procedure is appropriate for both individuals and groups. Here is an example of group action:

A class of five-year-old children learns that the music teacher introduced the first graders to the schools' expensive percussion instruments during their regularly scheduled music time. They want to know why they cannot participate in music with the percussion instruments. Their teacher, Mr. Paschal, suggests that the children write a letter to the music teacher to find out if her policy could be reviewed and perhaps changed. Mr. Paschal assisted the children to make the points they felt were necessary to have the policy changed.

The music teacher visited the kindergartners and explained to them that her goals in music education were to focus on their singing ability. "We'll work with the musical instruments next year," she explained. The children were disappointed, but Mr. Paschal nurtured them and told them that sometimes negotiation does not always mean you will "win your point of view."

Keys to Effective Classroom Management

◆   Some rules are non-negotiable. In this instance, children need to learn that "no" means no.

Learning Turn-Taking

The Issue

Early in the school year, young children will need to learn about turn-taking.

Overview

Young children may not have had experience with taking turns. In classrooms, materials and equipment are limited, and children must learn to take turns.

Goal

◆ To help children learn, with continual reminders, about taking turns

Solutions

The responsibility of taking turns could become a cornerstone of one of the class rules. Many scenarios in the classroom require turn taking, such as:

◆ playing with classroom material and equipment

◆ drinking from the water fountain

◆ lining up at the door (for entrance or departure)

◆ lining up to get on the school bus or van

◆ taking turns in various classroom centers

◆ talking during Circle Time

◆ sitting by the teacher during lunch

◆ special activities with the teacher (dictating a story or art projects that require adult assistance)

◆ taking turns with assigned classroom chores

◆ being the designated messenger during the day or week

Keys to Effective Classroom Management

◆ Some children may need you to demonstrate how to take turns to know what the concept means.

Learning to Make Decisions

The Issue

Andy was in the Home Living Center saying, "I want an egg. No, I don't want an egg. Yes, I want an egg. No, I don't want an egg." In a few minutes, he started his repetitions again, causing his teacher to chuckle silently. She recognized that this ritual was his self-talk activity for learning how to make decisions (Bodrova and Leong, 1995).

Overview

Decision-making processes begin in the early years. Making decisions when children are young helps them make appropriate decisions when they are adults.

Goal

◆ To support children in making their own decisions

Solutions

Giving children an opportunity to make decisions when they are young helps them learn this vital skill. The following are tips for planning decision-making situations:

◆ **Initially, children need a choice between two objects or events.**
   Examples include:
   • "Jackie, do you want me to read you a book or do you want to put together a puzzle?"
   • "Do you want to go to outdoors with all of the children, or do you want to stay in the classroom and listen to your CD? You won't be alone, because Ms. Patsy will stay with you."

◆ **Ensure the choices are equal, not artificial.**
   Appropriate Choices
   • "You can stay in the circle with your classmates, or you can go play with the Legos."
   • "Mickey, you are having difficulty playing in the Home Living Center with your friends. Your choices now are the Art Center and Grocery Store."

   Inappropriate Choices
   • "You can stay in the circle, or you can sit in this chair behind the circle."
   • "Mickey, you are having difficulty playing in the Home Living Center with your friends. Your choices now are to sit in the time-out chair or to go to the Book Corner."

◆ **Place no value on the choices children receive.**
   Appropriate Choices
   • "Today we are going to vote about whether we will go to the park on Friday or whether we'll attend the parade downtown." (No value is placed on the choice children make.)
   • "Brad, you have a choice between the Art Center or the Book Corner."

   Inappropriate Choices
   • "Today we are going to vote about whether we will go to the park on Friday or whether we'll attend the parade downtown where we'll see horses, clowns, and beautiful floats." (The parade choice is described in a more appealing way.)
   • "Brad, you have a choice between the Art Center or the Book Corner. I know you always like the Art Center, and I've added some fingerpaint today."

- **Make sure that children follow through on their choices.**
  - "Mickey, you chose to go to the Art Center, so you should not have returned to the Home Living Center. What do you need to do to correct this situation?"
  - "Brad, I'm surprised to find you here in the Book Corner. You told me you were going to the Art Center. What happened?"
- **Ensure that children are able to follow through with the choices they have made.**
  - "The vote this morning was 12 to four to go downtown to the parade on Friday. Let's talk about the things we need to do to plan this trip."
  - "You chose to play with the Legos today instead of coming to Circle Time. Show me what you accomplished."
- **Recognize that children, like adults, do change their minds occasionally.**
  - "Okay, Brad, I understand your decision to change your mind about the Art Center. Next time, would you tell me so that I will understand your viewpoint? What are you reading here in the Book Corner?"
- **Help children understand that some choices are good, while others are not.**
  - "Class, let's spend some time this morning talking about healthy food choices and unhealthy food choices."
  - "Mitch, taking another person's toy is a choice you made, but is it the best choice you could have made?"
- **Give instruction to children about outcomes of choices.**
  - "Class, you decided today that you wanted to go to the parade on Friday. What are some of the important things we have to think about in getting to the parade?" You may need to help children brainstorm about transportation, crossing busy intersections, safety, and finding a good place to see the parade.

Center Time is designed to give children choices and make decisions. See page 59 "Providing Choices" for more information about planning choices for children.

Keys to Effective Classroom Management

- Children usually make emotionally based choices. The goal is to help them move toward intellectually based choices.

Understanding Others' Viewpoints

The Issue

Preschoolers think about themselves first because of their egocentric perspective. As a consequence, they may hurt others physically and emotionally without thinking about the repercussions of their behaviors.

Overview

Young children need information about others' viewpoints, including the feelings of others and how others comprehend events. Developing a strong classroom community is a cornerstone of the preschool years.

Goal

◆ To help children become more capable of understanding others' viewpoints

Solutions

Teaching children about the viewpoint of others is rather easy. Here are some classroom examples:

◆ **One approach is to verbalize children's feelings to others.**

‣ "Bonnie, look how upset Ozzy is. I noticed you took her book, and this made her angry. Now that we know the problem, how can we solve it?"

‣ "Claire, Monica cries when you tell her that she cannot play with you and your friends. Let's talk about some solutions to this situation."

‣ "Howie, you are going around the room punching your friends in the arm. How do you think they feel when you do that?"

- **Another approach is to help children verbalize their own feelings.**
  - "Doug, King has something to tell you about how you treated him today in the Block Center. King, what do you want to say?"
  - "Phil, I can tell you are upset with Buddy. I'll go with you to talk to him about your anger."
  - "Heather, when you stop crying, we can visit with Brandie to talk with her about taking your art supplies."
- **A third approach is to allow children to verbalize their own feelings without adult intervention.**
  - Mrs. Klingbail notices that Hannah and Brittany are having a disagreement. She overhears Hannah say, "Just leave me alone. You always bite me!"
  - "Hey, stop that!" Mrs. Black heard from the Block Center. She turned around and smiled to herself that Goeff and Craig seemed to be working out their differences.
  - Ms. Brashears acknowledged Brandon with a private comment. "I noticed that you and Lance were having a tug of war over one of the wheel toys, but you worked out how you will share the toy."
- **A fourth approach is to plan group discussions about hurtful words and physical actions that are harmful to others.**
  - "Let's say that Buster wants a puzzle that Bryce is putting together. What is the best way for him to get the puzzle?"
  - "Today, I noticed that some children in our class were throwing toys instead of playing with them. Why is this not a good thing to do in our classroom?"
  - "During outdoor time, I heard some of the children in our class calling others bad names. Why is calling people names inappropriate? What do we need to do to correct this situation?"
- **Send home newsletters or individual messages soliciting support from parents to encourage their child to think of other children's feelings and points of view.**

Keys to Effective Classroom Management

- Learning and understanding the viewpoint of others is an ongoing challenge. Children need frequent instruction about including others and being sensitive to children's feelings.

Learning How to Get What You Want

The Issue

Children who take others' toys and supplies, or who charge into a play setting inappropriately are challenges. How can you help them learn to get what they want without behaving aggressively?

Overview

The use of diplomacy and negotiation skills is as important for young children as it is for adults.

Goals

- To teach children to become more comfortable with asking for what they want, and to help them become more comfortable with negative responses

Solutions

The following are suggestions for assisting children in getting what they want:

- **Model appropriate behaviors for children.**
  - "Let's talk to Paul about playing with the Etch-a-Sketch for awhile. He's had it most of the morning."
- **Assist children in using appropriate behaviors.**
  - "I'll go with you to ask Jeremy if you can use the tricycle when he's finished with it. Will that help you?"
  - "When you want a new toy, the best way to get it is to save your money so you can buy it. I'll help you write a note to your mom about what you want. Are there jobs you can do around the house to earn money?"
- **Help children negotiate a satisfactory result.**
  - "Paul says he wants to play with the Etch-a-Sketch for about 10 more minutes. I'll watch and tell you both when 10 minutes has passed."
  - "Michele, I know you want to finish the book. Would you make sure that Kimmy has it when you finish it? Kimmy, how do you feel about that?"

- **Suggest other activities, if necessary.**
  - "Todd, the tricycle is not available right now. Three more names are on the turn-taking list. Let's find another toy you can play with or you can play at the sand table."
  - "Melinda, I know you want Mary's doll, but it belongs to her. She brought it from home. Let's find another doll in the classroom you can play with."
- **Have group discussions with children about getting what they want.**
  - "All of us want things we like. Let's talk about some strategies for getting what you want. (Older preschoolers will be able to brainstorm appropriate approaches: saving money to buy what you want, asking for specific objects for birthdays or as holiday gifts, going to garage sales, and so on.)
  - "Children, when you decide what you want, why do you sometimes have to wait to get it?" (Older preschoolers will be able to understand the concept of delayed gratification).
- **Hold private discussions with children.**
  - "Chris, I know you're upset because you didn't get to go to the library today. Let's talk about your options while you're in the classroom."
  - "I noticed you like the fancy markers in the Art Center. Have you started saving your money so you can buy some for home?"
- **Help children deal with the reality of the situation.**
  - "In our class, we set a limit on the number of children who can play in each center. Right now there are three children in the Puppet Center. Can you find another center where you can play?"
  - "I know your best friend is not here today, but you can still choose an activity in the classroom instead of sitting here alone."

Keys to Effective Classroom Management

- Telling children some personal experiences about getting or not getting what you want will help them understand that they cannot always have what they want.

Learning How to Become Part of a Play Setting

The Issue

Some children do not have much experience playing with other children before they come to school. They need instruction about playing with others.

Overview

Children will eventually learn that other children do not like it when they aggressively enter play settings. They will learn to become subtle with entrance behaviors and more willing to participate in the "give and take" required to play with others.

Goal

◆ To teach children about entering a play setting, which helps teach them social skills they may not have learned in previous experiences

Solutions

Recommendations for helping children become part of a play setting include:

◆ **Model appropriate behaviors for children.**
  - "You know, when I want to join a group of friends, I go to them and say, 'Can I join you for a while?' Have you tried asking them if you can play?"
  - "Come with me. I'll show you how to become part of the Home Living Center play. Say, 'Hi, Sarah and Flo, I want to play with you. Can I be one of the sisters?'"

◆ **Assist children in becoming players in play situations.**
  - "Mary, I'll go with you to find out if the group in the Home Living Center will let you join their play."
  - "Jackie told me that she wants to play with the playdough, too. There's room here at the table. What do you think?"

- **Help children negotiate play entrances.**
  - "You know, Clarissa, these children are pretending to be a family. Is there a family member you could pretend to be? Why don't you suggest being one of the sisters?"
  - "Mary Frances has suggested she might be a pet in the family. Does that seem acceptable to you?"
  - "Roy is a great bridge builder, and he wants to join your play in the Block Center. Will you give him a chance to build a tall bridge?"
- **Introduce negotiation skills to children if necessary.**
  - "Yes, Roy, I heard the children in the Block Center say 'no,' but did you tell them what a great bridge builder you are?"
  - "Mary Frances, did you suggest that you could be a puppy in the family? The children in the Home Living Center may not need more sisters, but have you tried asking about being a puppy?"
- **If children are unsuccessful, help them accept the reality of the situation.**
  - "Well, I can understand why the children in the Home Living Center said 'no,' because there are too many children in the family already. Is there something else you can choose until a place becomes available in the Home Living Center?"
  - "Play time is almost over, and it looks like the tricycles are being used for the full time. What can you do instead?"
- **Suggest alternative play activities, if necessary.**
  - "When I have trouble finding someone to go to the movies with me, I just go by myself. Playing alone can be fun."
  - "Vicki was looking for someone to play Legos with her earlier. Why don't you ask her if she will play with you?"

Keys to Effective Classroom Management

- Some children are content to play alone. Socialization skills emerge as children discover the types of play they enjoy most.

Interpersonal Problem-Solving Skills

The Issue

Mrs. Smith noticed early in the school year that friction erupted almost every time Clay and Johnny were together in any center. They would yell at one another and occasionally hit one another. She decided they needed some instruction about solving their own problems.

Overview

Intervening and stopping fights is a one-time solution, but teaching children their own interpersonal problem-solving skills is beneficial to them in the long run.

Goal

◆   To teach children a strategy for solving interpersonal problems and to help them practice the strategy to learn it well

---

Solving a Problem

1. Name the problem.
2. Talk about the problem.
3. Talk about solutions.
4. Agree on one solution.
5. Try out the solution.
6. Ask if the solution works.

Solutions

These are the steps Mrs. Smith followed to help Clay and Johnny:

◆   **Step 1: Help children recognize that a problem exists.**
    "Okay, young men, let's stop the fighting. I notice that when you two are together, you seem to start fighting. Let's talk about the problem."

◆   **Step 2: Ask each child involved to tell what he believes the problem is.**
    "Johnny, what do you believe the problem is between you and Clay?"
    "Clay, do you think what John is saying is correct? What is your thinking?"

◆ **Step 3: Once the problem is defined, generate a solution to the problem.**
    "Johnny, how do you think you can solve this problem?"
    "Clay, what are your ideas about a solution?"

◆   **Step 4: Agree on a solution to the problem.**
    "I think you two have generated a good solution. Changing centers when you're both angry would prevent your fighting. Let's try that for a few days to determine if it solves the problem."

◆   **Step 5: Reassess the problem at another time and brainstorm alternative strategies if necessary.**
    "Johnny and Clay, I've noticed that you are getting along better when you play in centers. Do you think your plan is working?"

◆   **Step 6: Review the steps in problem solving and ask children to use the strategy when they have problems in other relationships.**
    "Let's review what we did to solve the problem you had. Can you follow the same steps in other situations?"

Some teachers post a chart (see box on the left) on the classroom wall that defines the steps in solving a problem. This strategy is an excellent one for all children to know.

Keys to Effective Classroom Management

◆   Children will need numerous demonstrations of a problem-solving strategy before they are completely comfortable with using it.

Learning to Control Oneself

The Issue

Zane threw temper tantrums and lashed out at his friends when he couldn't have his way. His disruptive behavior caused chaos for the entire class, and his teacher observed he was becoming an outcast in the classroom.

Overview

Although Zane's teacher had talked to him about cooperative behaviors, his tantrums continued. Children can and must learn self-control. What was the teacher to do to help him solve his problem?

Goal

◆ To continue to teach children as many strategies as necessary to help them learn self-control

Solutions

When children such as Zane demonstrate disruptive behaviors after normal procedures are followed, try these techniques:

◆ Teach children a self-control strategy. Ask them to repeat to a certain phrase over and over again, "I will keep my hands to myself," or "I can stay calm."

◆ Encourage children to remove themselves from the play setting when they feel they are losing control.

◆ Develop a private cueing signal with specific children who have a temper problem. Catch their eyes and give them an "A-OK" signal if it appears they are managing themselves. If not, a head nod indicating your concern might be appropriate.

◆ If the problem continues, consider writing a contract with children. Provide a special reward if children can remember to control themselves for a reasonable period of time, for example, for one day. If they meet the contract, write a new contract extending the time to two or three days—whatever is appropriate for each child.

◆ If necessary, each morning ask the more volatile children what they will do when they feel like they are losing control.

◆ Make positive comments when children have controlled themselves during playtime. These comments can be public or private. Notes home to parents might also be a good idea.

Keys to Effective Classroom Management

◆ If classroom strategies are not working, suggest play therapy or other professional intervention to the child's parents.

◆ Some children do not respond to classroom discussions and suggestions. Continue to work with individuals who need extra patience and expertise with behavioral problems.

Learning How to Relax

The Issue

Raymond's teacher noticed he was about to erupt into one of his high-pitched squeals of stress as he put a puzzle together. She moved to him quickly, so she could hold him close and comfort him to prevent the loud scream.

Overview

Not only will children become less stressed if you follow some of these suggestions, but they will learn personal strategies for becoming de-stressed.

Goal

◆ To provide a variety of techniques to help children calm themselves

Solutions

The following techniques can help children learn to relax:

◆ Calm the child by talking to him in a soothing manner and holding him close, if necessary.

◆ Ask the child to take deep breaths. Say to him, "You seem to be stressed. Let's get rid of your stress. Breathe deeply. Here, watch me do it, and then you try it."

◆ Ask the child if he knows when he is stressed. Suggest options for reducing the stress. (One of the following techniques should be beneficial.)

◆ Take the child by the hand and walk away from the stressful situation. Say, "When I feel stressed, I walk around a few minutes. That usually helps me calm down."

◆ Demonstrate physical activities the child can do to calm himself, such as rubbing the back of his neck or temples or asking someone to massage his shoulders and back.

◆ Tell the child to hum or sing to himself to alleviate stress.

◆ Introduce group activities that will help all children to eliminate stress, such as lying on the floor and breathing deeply, closing one's eyes and using calming visual scenes, such as beach scenes or beautiful flower gardens.

◆ Have a rocking chair in the classroom that children can use when they feel stressed.

◆ Ensure that children are adequately fed and that they don't get thirsty. Meeting their physical needs eases stress.

◆ Follow the usual classroom routine. Stress occurs when children are not following their normal habits and schedules.

Keys to Effective Classroom Management

◆ Some of the stressful events in children's lives are beyond the control of the classroom. Talk to parents, too, about helping children avoid stress.

Handling Disappointment

The Issue

Living with disappointment is an issue that all people face, whether they are adults or children. Most adults have self-protective strategies that help them when they experience disappointment.

Overview

Learning to accept disappointment is part of learning to live one's life. The truth is harsh, but children need experiences with disappointment to become functionally healthy adolescents and adults. Learning to cope with disappointment at younger ages eases the transition to adulthood.

Goal

◆ To help children respond positively when you teach them to understand disappointments

Solutions

Consider these steps:

1. Talk to the child to learn the source of his disappointment (this may be obvious from previous observation).
2. Explain why the situation exists. For example, "We only have one wagon on the playground, and Olga and Melinda are playing with it right now."
3. Ask if another choice might be satisfactory (or suggest another choice).
4. If the child agrees to another choice, the problem is resolved. However, some children will continue to pout or cry. Explain that pouting or crying will not change the situation. You may have to say, "You're making yourself unhappy when you could be happy by playing with another toy."

Keys to Effective Classroom Management

◆ Helping children with this problem may take multiple experiences with disappointment.

Handling Tattling

The Issue

Children tell on each other for different reasons. Regardless of their reasons for tattling, it is a source of frustration for adults.

Overview

To eliminate tattling, give children a response that they can use to stop another child's negative behavior.

Goal

◆ To teach children what to say when the behavior of others bothers them

Solutions

The following are a few responses to try to teach tattlers to resolve the situation:

◆ Alison came to her teacher and said, "Marty hit me."
   The response: "Tell Marty that you don't like to be hit."

◆ Caitlin reported that Jeremy said the "f" word.
   The response: "Did you tell him that his language is not appropriate in our classroom?"

◆ When Larry said to his teacher, "Leeann stole my pencil," his teacher asked, "Did you see her steal your pencil?" When he responded "yes," his teacher told him to go to Leeann and ask her to return his pencil.

◆ "Devon isn't building the bridge right," tattled Abby.
   The response: "Remind him of the rules for the Block Corner," responded his teacher.

◆ "Joe used a bad word, Teacher," Barnett exclaimed as he came in from the playground.
   The response: "What did you say to him when he used the bad word?" "I told him that the word wasn't a good one to use." "Good for you!"

Keys to Effective Classroom Management

◆ Helping children become more assertive with classroom problems solves the need to tattle.

Preschool Classroom Management

Handling Children Who Use Foul Language

The Issue

Donny's use of four-letter words was shocking to his preschool teacher. He used the "f" word in almost every sentence he uttered. Though Mrs. Dubois talked to him about his inappropriate language, he continued to use it throughout his school day.

Overview

Not all parents tell children that some language is unacceptable. Most teachers do not allow the use of foul language in the classroom. Just as children need to control their emotions, they must also learn to control their language. Eventually, children will omit words that are considered "bad." However, the extinction of this negative habit may take several weeks or months.

Goal

◆ To use strategies to eliminate the use of foul language in the classroom

Solutions

Working with young children to eliminate foul language may require several strategies, such as:

◆ First, talk to the child individually about what is acceptable and unacceptable language in the classroom. Say, "This language is not acceptable at school."

◆ If the problem continues, talk to the child's parents and elicit their assistance.

◆ Some language is so entrenched that children are not aware they are using it. Set up a system of rewards for the child to help extinguish the negative behavior. "If you go an hour without using a bad word, I will put a button in this baby food jar. If you get five buttons today, you get a special certificate to take home. Your mother will be glad to see it." Or, you could use the following incentive: "If you get five buttons, you can choose your favorite toy to take home overnight." Use the "just one more" technique described on page 85 to lengthen the rewards system.

◆ If other children report the child's bad language, tell them what to say, such as, "Hey, that word isn't a good one to use here at school."

Keys to Effective Classroom Management

◆ Helping children develop socially acceptable skills is important for their development as future citizens of the community.

When Children Lie

The Issue

Mrs. Gonzales was surprised when she overheard one of her children telling another child in the school that they never had snack time. "Why, Jacob, I serve snack every day. You choose not to eat what I give you, but we do indeed have snack."

Overview

Children learn about honesty and dishonesty in the early years. Mrs. Gonzales interpreted Jacob's discussion with his schoolmate as being a lie. Young children often define the worlds they live in from their perspective. Though Mrs. Gonzales provided graham crackers and milk every morning, Jacob did not choose to eat the snack and interpreted his choice as the class having no snack.

Goal

◆ To help young children learn about honesty and deal with the consequences of their behavior

Solutions

When children appear to be lying, follow these steps for helping them with this unacceptable habit:

◆ Look at the situation from the child's viewpoint. Is what the child saying a lie or a misinterpretation of life's events?

◆ Is the child being imaginative? Some creative children enjoy making up stories. Help them realize that you recognize the story for what it is—a fun, made-up story about their experiences.

◆ If the child is lying deliberately, correct the statement with a matter-of-fact statement. In a private moment, talk to the child about lying and discuss the consequences of lying.

◆ If the problem appears to be one the whole group is having, tell them the story of "The Boy Who Cried Wolf."

Keys to Effective Classroom Management

◆ Provide an appropriate role model for children by always telling the truth yourself. In addition, remember to keep promises you make to the children.

Working With Children Who Steal

The Issue

Mrs. Batiste discovered that she had a thief in her classroom. Danielle reported that her snack money was gone, and Roberta indicated that her new marker was missing. Mrs. Batiste believed that the children were honest, but she also knows that young children do occasionally steal. She wanted to find out who was responsible.

Overview

Some children steal during the early years. Sometimes, their personal desires will outweigh their ability to understand that possessions belong to someone else. They see a prized possession, and they take it—especially if it does not appear to belong to someone else.

Goal

◆   To help children learn not to take the property of others

Solutions

Here are some tips for discovering who a culprit is and reclaiming stolen objects without placing a heavy sense of guilt on the child who took the object:

◆   Children who steal do not always hide their stolen goods very well. Look around the classroom to discover the missing objects.

◆   Think about a time when one child might have been in the classroom alone. Most likely, this was an opportunity for the child to pick up an item that belonged to someone else.

◆   When stolen property is found, quietly ask the suspect if the object might belong to another child who is missing the stolen item.

◆   Remember that an important American principle is that the accused is innocent until proven guilty. If the child admits to his misdeed, the consequence of his action is that he will need to return the stolen item to its owner.

◆   If the child lies to cover his actions, investigate further by talking to the child's parent.

◆   When a child has, in fact, stolen something, talk in private with him about taking other's property. Remind the child that some toys look alike, and perhaps he has mistaken someone else's toy for his own.

◆   Collaborate with parents and the child to take away a privilege as a consequence for having stolen someone else's belongings. Use diplomacy with parents. Talking to parents about children's egocentric thinking and their need to respect others' possessions will alleviate this difficult situation.

Keys to Effective Classroom Management

◆   Most children are going to feel guilty even if their actions go undetected. Private discussions with individuals about their thefts without placing blame are necessary to prevent this problem from reoccurring.

Working With Children Who Masturbate

The Issue

Ms. Perkins noticed that Felicia had begun masturbating. Because of Felicia's age (three years), her teacher did not worry about it as a sign of serious underlying emotional problems, an issue that might signal a need to worry if observed in older children. First she decided to divert Felicia's attention from the activity, knowing that she might need to address the masturbation issue if it continued.

Overview

Three-year-old children who begin experimentation with masturbation are in the normal range of development. Young children may need to understand that they should not feel shame or guilt participating in a pleasurable experience.

Goal

◆ To help young children who masturbate understand that it is an activity that should occur in the privacy of their bedrooms

Solutions

Steps for helping children who masturbate include:

1. Try diverting attention from masturbation by giving the child something to do with his hands (play with a ball, hold a toy, or participate in an art activity).

2. If masturbation continues openly, pull the child aside and talk to him or her about masturbation as an activity that needs to be conducted within the privacy of his bedrooms.

3. Avoid shaming or belittling the child for participating in an activity that feels pleasurable. Children should understand that masturbation is normal, but it should be a private experience.

4. Talk to the child's parents if the masturbation continues. Tell them how you are handling the problem in the classroom, and encourage them to explain to the child that masturbation is a private experience.

5. Children will outgrow the need to masturbate if adults have a developmental perspective of the issue. If masturbation continues in the classroom, a deeper problem may exist, and you should prepare to contact professionals who can help you, the parents, and the child solve the problem.

Keys to Effective Classroom Management

◆ Older preschoolers who masturbate openly may have serious underlying emotional problems or be a victim of abuse (Hendrick, 2002). Be observant of other signs that might indicate that sexual abuse is occurring. Follow state and school guidelines for reporting your suspicions.

Having Group Meetings to Discuss Classroom Problems

The Issue

If you notice that a classroom rule infraction occurs again and again, take time to talk with the group about the problem.

Overview

When many children are actively involved in inappropriate behavior, a group meeting may remind them of the reason why a rule is established. A group meeting allows children to talk about alternative behaviors. Children begin to remind one another when the inappropriate behavior occurs.

Goal

♦ To help children learn to discuss a problem as a group and come up with options to solve it

Solutions

Call the children together in a group as soon as possible after you notice that one of the classroom rules is being broken consistently. Describe the problem to the children, and ask them to remember why the rule is in place. If children cannot remember why the rule exists, remind them.

Then ask the children to brainstorm steps for ensuring that the rule is followed. Writing these on a chart might be helpful for some groups of children. The next day, remind the children of their group discussion and ask them to remember the choices they have for following the classroom rules.

Observe children as they play, and remind individuals, if necessary.

Keys to Effective Classroom Management

♦ Occasionally, the rule is not a workable one. For example, children love to throw balls, whether they are in the classroom or on the playground. In this case, removing balls as classroom play objects is a solution if children throwing balls in the classroom either bothers you or is unsafe.

Learning to Care for Others

The Issue

If children have had few experiences in groups of children, their ability to care for one another might be limited. As a general rule, young children are egocentric, thinking of themselves first before they think about others.

Overview

Helping children become less egocentric as they move through the preschool years is an important teaching goal.

Goal

◆ To develop a "caring community" concept in your classroom

Solutions

The following are recommendations for helping children become less egocentric:

◆ Model showing interest in all of the children in the classroom.

◆ Explain to children why someone is absent or why a child is crying, to help them understand that everyone has similar emotions and problems.

◆ Write a class card to a child who is in the hospital and encourage individual children to do the same (or make a card in the Art Center).

◆ Demonstrate to children appropriate responses when an absent child returns after being away from the classroom.

◆ Read books that show children caring about others.

◆ Comment favorably when you observe children demonstrating care for their classmates.

◆ Ask parents if they have observed children caring for others (their siblings, for example), and tell the class what you have heard from their parents.

Keys to Effective Classroom Management

◆ Maria Montessori taught her children the "Do unto others as you would have them do unto you" concept (Standing, 1984; Orem, 1974; Montessori, 1965). Though embedded in Christianity, this spiritual principle transcends all religions by focusing on caring for oneself and others in the same manner.

Teaching Altruism

The Issue

The foundation of children's positive relations with others begins in early childhood. How do teachers convey altruism?

Overview

Most adults choose work and personal pursuits because they enjoy these activities. Reaching out and helping others is altruistic and makes adults feel good. Learning altruism begins during childhood, and wise teachers will model altruism and encourage it from the children in their classroom.

Goals

- To identify and encourage the development of altruistic feelings and give them a name

Solutions

Suggestions for helping children learn altruism include:

- Talk about how you feel when you help your friends.
- Use a group discussion to talk about how children feel when they help others.
- When you observe a child doing something special for a friend, ask him to tell how he is feeling.
- Encourage parents to talk to their children about the altruistic feelings they have.
- Invite a community volunteer to talk about what he does to help people in trouble. Ask him to discuss his altruistic feelings.

Keys to Effective Classroom Management

- Altruism is an abstract principle that has its roots in positive feelings that children have in the early childhood years. Help children sort out their feelings and discover altruism.

Avoiding Negativity: No, Don't, and Stop

The Issue

Working with young children can become very demanding emotionally. You may find yourself caught in a cycle of negativity. When you become negative, children are likely to become negative and oppositional as well.

Overview

Consider the language that you use in the classroom. When you find that you frequently use "no," "don't," and "stop," change your language to reflect a more positive approach.

Goals

◆ To monitor the use of negative language patterns, to decrease the use of negative directives in the classroom, and to use positive directions when addressing classroom concerns

Solutions

Some of the ways that you can monitor your language with young children include the following:

◆ Focus on the most stressful time of the day when you are most likely to use negative language.

◆ Count the number of times that you say, "no," "don't," and "stop" in a morning or afternoon. To do this, you can tally with a sticky note and pencil, or you can transfer pennies from one pocket to the other.

◆ Consider alternative positive phrases that can be used to guide children (see chart below).

Suggested Alternative Phrases

Negative Words	Positive Words
No	Wait
	We'll see.
	Be careful.
	Remember to _____.
Don't	Let's go over here.
	Watch out for _____.
	Let's do it this way.
	Please help me to _____.
Stop	_____ are not for _____.
	(Chairs are not for throwing.)
	Let's calm down.
	Come here, please.
	(child's name), what are the rules?
	What do you need to do?

- If you find that you are using these terms more than five times each morning, set a personal goal to reduce the number of time you use these terms. Continue counting and recording your use of "no," "don't," and "stop."
- As you monitor your words, consider your facial expressions. Eye contact can say a great deal.
- Reward yourself with something you enjoy or a special treat when you are able to get your use of these negative directives under control.
- Rephrase the directives to children positively. Instead of "no," "don't," and "stop," use these directions instead:
  - Remember to…
  - We need to…
  - Morgan (name of child), wait…
  - Let's do this…
  - Here's what we need to do…
  - What do you need to do?

Keys to Effective Classroom Management

- It is always more effective if you can pre-empt the behavior rather than react to it when it occurs. If you are aware of children's behavior and what types of problems are likely to happen, you can remind children of what they need to do before they encounter the problem. This avoids the need to use negative terms such as "no," "don't," and "stop." When you have a positive attitude it helps children to maintain a positive attitude, as well.
- At first you might be surprised at the number of times that you say "no," "don't," or "stop." If you find that you need to use these terms in emergency situations constantly throughout the day, then you need to examine the classroom environment. Make sure the classroom is safe enough for children's exploration and active play without constant reminders or reprimands.

Putting It Into Practice: Tamara

The principles supporting this narrative are:

♦ Classroom management requires teachers to deal with individual problems.

♦ When one technique fails, try another.

♦ Some children respond quickly, while others require a longer time to respond.

♦ Involve the family as much as possible when dealing with a child's problems.

♦ Sharing personal experiences will facilitate children's understanding of their own problems.

♦ Children may need instruction about expressing their feelings before they can verbalize their needs and concerns.

♦ Professional assistance beyond the classroom is necessary on occasion.

♦ Patience and good humor are essential to success.

The "clean-up song" was over, and Barbara called Tamara to leave the Home Living Center because it was time to come to Circle Time. Tamara began to whine as Barbara called her again. The next thing she knew, Tamara was on floor crying, doll in hand. "No! No! Doe-wanna," yelled Tamara. As Barbara approached Tamara to take her hand and redirect her to the circle, Tamara threw herself on the floor, kicking and screaming in a full-blown tantrum. These episodes seemed to happen all too frequently with Tamara in Barbara's classroom of three-year-olds. Barbara decided that something had to change, so she went to a two-day workshop where she learned many new strategies to deal with problem behavior. She also learned that there was no magic solution, and that behavior change takes knowledge, time, energy, and creativity.

Barbara began by observing Tamara during the day for a week. She wrote down when Tamara threw tantrums, what seemed to set them off, what was happening before the tantrum, and what happened afterward. Barbara learned that Tamara threw tantrums primarily during transition times. Most of the time the pay-off for the tantrum was getting to play with toys or getting some activity that she wanted—and not having to change the ongoing activity. Tamara's actions had a definite pattern: whining, then verbal refusal, then throwing herself on the floor, and finally a full-blown tantrum with kicking and screaming. At each step of the way Tamara expected to achieve her goal, and if she did not get what she wanted she escalated her behavior.

The first step that Barbara took was to develop a class schedule using picture cards. She discussed the daily plans with the children at the beginning of the day during planning time. Before beginning an activity in the day (circle, centers, playground, work time, snack), Barbara showed the associated picture and they planned what they would do next. She also set a timer to let the children know when it was time to clean up. When she finished the clean-up song, she started talking about the next activity. She kept her tone of voice positive and playful. She raced with Tamara to see who could pick up the most toys in centers. Barbara commented on how well Tamara was able to pick up toys.

On the playground, Barbara started an exercise routine with a small group of children (including Tamara) before it was time to go inside. They

imitated Barbara as she jumped, ran in place, stretched, kicked, and clapped. Then they followed as she bunny-hopped toward the gate to head to the classroom. Barbara reminded the children that when they were finished at the worktable that they would have snacks. Altogether, these strategies seemed to work well with Tamara. Tantrums were occurring much less frequently at school.

At the parent conference Mr. and Mrs. Clark, Tamara's parents, reported that her tantrums were still frequent at home. Barbara and the parents were still concerned about Tamara's delayed language development. She spoke only in two-word sentences and was approaching her fourth birthday. Also, she left off word endings and was able to pronounce a limited number of speech sounds. Barbara and the parents had hoped that the language-rich experiences in her preschool classroom would improve her vocabulary and sentence structure. Even though her tantrums had improved at school, she still had difficulty "using her words" to make her needs known. Tamara's parents decided to have her evaluated by a speech-language pathologist. After this evaluation, Tamara began speech therapy for language and articulation delays.

Tamara's mother, Mrs. Clark, observed unobtrusively in the classroom to see how Barbara dealt with Tamara's behavior. It was a real surprise to see how well Tamara followed the routine and directions with the classroom. When she talked with Barbara about Tamara's behavior, Barbara described how Tamara usually had trouble with transitions, and how she escalated from whining to throwing herself on the floor to a full-blown tantrum. Barbara also related that tantrums could usually be avoided at the whining stage. Barbara discussed the classroom modifications that she had made to avoid Tamara's tantrums: a picture schedule, imitation exercises, making cleanup a game, setting a timer, and discussing the schedule before changes in activity.

At home Tamara threw tantrums to get things that she wanted such as toys, food, or activities. At the store checkout, she would whine for candy and her mother would tell her "no." Then she would cry, and if that did not work she would begin kicking and screaming. By that time everyone in the store was looking at her. Then her mother would tell her, "If you will stop crying then you can have the candy." Tamara would quiet down and get the candy. She had learned that "no" means "keep trying" until you get what you want. After observing at school, Mrs. Clark realized what was happening and changed her tactics completely. She told Tamara that she

(continued on the next page)

could have a treat when they finished shopping only if she was polite and did not cry. If she cried or whined she would not get a treat. While shopping she reminded Tamara of this. At first she had to remove Tamara from the store and go home when Tamara threw a tantrum. After the second trip home, Tamara learned that she would not get a treat if she cried or whined. Later, when Tamara began whining at the store, her mother only had to ask her if she needed to go home. She was able to quiet down and accept "no" for an answer. It was harder on her mother at first, but in the long run it paid off for both of them. Mrs. Clark continued to work with Tamara at home, and made sure that Tamara was not rewarded for her tantrums. Barbara also continued to work with her at school, and Tamara's progress in speech therapy enabled her to better express herself verbally. Even though Tamara still resorted to tantrums on occasion, she was definitely making progress at both school and home.

Preschool Classroom Management

Parent Partnerships

Chapter 6

Parents are the child's first teachers. Young children are totally dependent on others to meet their needs and teach them what they need to know. Because of the importance of the family in the life of children, teachers need to enlist their help in working with the children with challenging behavior. This chapter recognizes that families are diverse and may have parenting styles and values that are different from those of the teachers at school. There are strengths in those differences, and building a relationship with families is of mutual benefit to the teacher and the family. The assumption here is that teachers will work to develop a partnership rather than assume that the school is the "pool of wisdom" and that the parents are the "needy clients."

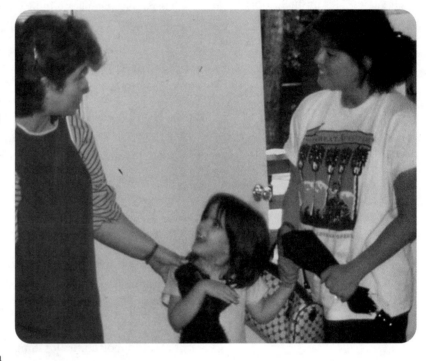

Much of this chapter focuses on communicating with parents. The child is the parent's most cherished treasure. If the parent thinks that the teacher is criticizing the child or does not like the child, then trouble will likely follow. This chapter also addresses family problems that affect the child and the school. Although the school is not in the position of providing therapy or social services, there is much that can be done to understand the problems, build a relationship, and work together to help the child. When schools and families work together it is a win-win situation. And the child is the one who is the biggest winner!

Honoring Diversity

The Issue

Families have different situations, cultures, values, and histories. Every family has its own story, and the child fits into the family in unique ways. Many times teachers come from entirely different backgrounds, values, and cultures than the children that they work with—and they expect families to conform to their values. This mismatch may lead to difficulties between the family and the school.

Overview

When you learn about families and their values, you are better able to work effectively with the child.

Goal

♦ To learn about the families in your class and their goals for the children. This knowledge will lead to respect for the families and their choices.

Solutions

When getting to know the families of the children in your class, consider the following:

♦ Recognize the fact that you have values that may be different from some of the families that you work with.

♦ Don't assume that your way is the right way or the best way.

♦ Learn about the fundamental values of the various racial and ethnic groups in the community where you work.

♦ Don't assume that all families from a specific racial or ethnic group fit one pattern: people are individuals, and they do not necessarily conform to any pattern; families are unique and may not have the same values as others in their racial or ethnic group.

♦ Understand and become aware of your own fundamental values and culture.

♦ Get to know people in your school or community who can help you to learn more about their culture.

♦ If families speak languages other than English, learn a few phrases in their language.

♦ Be aware that rapport takes time.

♦ Work with interpreters to improve communication with families when needed.

♦ Send home notes in the family language whenever possible.

♦ Be aware that family involvement may not be customary in the family's culture. This does not mean that they are not interested.

♦ Try to see the world from the point of view of the other person.

♦ Provide opportunities for families to make choices in how they participate in the classroom.

Keys to Effective Classroom Management

♦ Everyone sees the world through his or her own cultural blinders. All people are prisoners of their prejudices. Anything you can do to raise your sensitivity to other cultures will enable you to grow as a teacher and person. Some experiences that help you to know more about other cultures include friendships with people from various cultures, reading about many cultures, and travel.

Parenting Styles

The Issue

Families have different styles of interacting with children, one another, and the school. Some families may be formal, while others are more casual in their interactions. Other factors include the style of communication, discipline methods, the degree of control, the social place of children, and tolerance for child behaviors. There are numerous factors that are involved in the style of parenting.

Overview

To understand a child's behavior, it is helpful to be familiar with the parenting style of the family. The context of the school is very different from the context of the home, and it is critical to understand and respect the family. Understanding parenting styles is also important when enlisting the help of the family in dealing with a child's challenging behavior at school. You will have a better idea of what would be acceptable to the family and their role in the plan to change the child's behavior.

Goals

◆ To build relationships with families, and, therefore, be better able to interpret the child's behavior in the school setting, and to help the child improve her behavior at school

Solutions:

Some of the things to be aware of in considering the parenting style of the family are:

◆ Attitude toward discipline
◆ Communication among family members
◆ Family and school roles
◆ Roles within the family
◆ Willingness to work with "outsiders"
◆ Relationships and roles of siblings
◆ Respect and ideas about "personal" property
◆ Expectation of manners in children
◆ Attitude toward child communication
◆ Role of extended family members
◆ Tolerance for children's level of activity
◆ Degree of formality within the home
◆ Importance of routine and schedule

Keys to Effective Classroom Management

◆ The family is a complex system. Often family members will listen but will not act on your advice when the recommendations do not coincide with their parenting style.
◆ To develop effective partnerships with parents, acknowledge and respect both their culture and their parenting style.

111

Collaborative Relationships

The Issue

Often, a wide gulf exists between the "professionals" at school and the family. Many families believe that the teachers always know best. Teachers sometimes believe that their way is the best way or the only way to do things.

Overview

Collaborative relationships between the school and parents set the stage for effective problem solving to meet children's needs.

Goal

♦ To build collaborative school-family relationships to meet the needs of the children

Solutions

Consider the following when establishing and nurturing collaborative school-family relationships:

♦ Get to know the family in a comfortable setting through parent conferences, meetings, etc.

♦ Focus on the child and her needs—don't just tell parents what they need to do.

♦ Respect family preferences and values.

♦ Build a relationship of respect and trust over time.

♦ Provide opportunities for families to get to know one another.

♦ Enlist the parents' help when a child has a behavior problem.

♦ Brainstorm together using a problem-solving process:

1. Define the problem.
2. Brainstorm solutions
3. Consider the various solutions.
4. Select a potential solution.
5. Try it out.
6. Review the results.
7. Continue to consider other solutions if needed.

♦ Be aware that the family is the child's first teacher, and they know the child better than anyone else.

♦ Be knowledgeable about community resources that can assist families in meeting the child's needs.

Keys to Effective Classroom Management

♦ Consequences for behavior need to be natural, related to the behavior, and as immediate as possible. Avoid relying on parents to provide negative consequences that are far removed from problem behavior at school. If you rely on parents in this way, families come to dread the call from you—or worse yet, you start to blame the parents for not enacting consequences that deter the behavior. Parents and teachers need to work together to solve behavior problems, not enlist the family as the "enforcer."

Communicating With Parents

The Issue

Oral communication skills are very important when establishing a partnership with parents.

Overview

Parent partnerships are vital when working with children, especially those who have social and behavioral difficulties. Promote a positive relationship with parents when you talk with them.

Goal

◆ To be an effective oral communicator when working together with parents

Solutions

Consider the following when developing good communication skills with parents:

◆ First impressions are powerful. When meeting parents for the first time, make sure that you are respectful and child-focused.

◆ Time spent "up front" in establishing a relationship with parents is the first step in working together to solve behavior problems.

◆ If you need more time to talk individually with a parent, set up a time that is mutually convenient.

◆ Privacy is important when discussing child behavior problems.

◆ When talking about a child's behavior problem, solicit the parent's opinion and insights about what they think of the child's behavior.

◆ Pause and give the parent time to speak. If you are so busy talking the parent may stop listening or be unable to respond.

◆ Listening is just as important as speaking.

◆ Remember that eye contact is important.

◆ Be aware that your body language communicates just as much as your words.

◆ Your tone of voice also communicates just as much as words.

◆ Don't get defensive if the parent seems to be demanding or accusing. Listen first— respond later!

◆ Express your concerns about the child using "I" statements, such as "When ____ happens, I feel _____." (See page 115 for more information on using "I" Statements.) Avoid statements that sound accusing or blaming of parents.

◆ Be aware that it is difficult for many parents to talk about their child's problems: Parents may take criticism of their children very personally.

◆ Know that you are not always right and that it is okay to make mistakes—as well as to apologize.

Keys to Effective Classroom Management

◆ Sometimes teachers tend to speak to parents as they would one of the children in the class. Remember to "switch gears" and speak to parents as adults.

◆ Be aware that you may not always be as successful as you would like in communicating about a child and your need for support from the home to improve behavior. Effective problem solving is not a quick fix and requires time.

Listening Skills

The Issue

Being good listeners is not easy and takes lots of practice. Listening is a critical skill when building relationships with parents and others. Communication occurs when the listener and speaker are able to share their thoughts.

Overview

Adults can learn to become good listeners. Specific listening behaviors can be recognized, taught, and used. This will enable you and the family to build a relationship of understanding. An effective partnership with families requires communication between the teacher and parents. Families want to know that you care about their child. Listening to what they have to say is critical in building parent partnerships.

Goal

- To learn to use the skills that are important when listening to parents, which will result in improved communication and relationships with family members

Solutions

To become a good listener, or to refine your listening skills, consider these ideas:

- Be aware that effective listening is an active process.
- Whenever possible, arrange for a time and place where there are minimal distractions.
- Don't work on lesson preparations, art projects, or paperwork while you are talking with a parent.
- Clear your mind:
  - Focus on the speaker, not on all of the things that you need to do.
  - Focus on the speaker, not on the wonderful advice that you want to give them as soon as there is a break in the conversation.
- Keep your input to a minimum—don't monopolize the conversation.
- Prompt the speaker through nodding your head and verbal confirmations such as "yes", "okay", "I see", "uh-huh", etc.
- Avoid expressing value judgments, both positive and negative, while listening. Value judgments may be expressed later in the conversation if you are engaged in problem solving.
- Maintain eye contact with the speaker, but avoid a "stare down."
- Clarify points by paraphrasing what the speaker is saying. This allows the speaker to confirm or explain their thoughts further.
- Reflect back to the speaker how you understand the feelings they are expressing. For example, if the speaker is talking about a problem with the child's temper tantrums, you might say, "It sounds like you are really frustrated with all of Tommy's tantrums at home."
- Practice empathy. Make every effort to see the child and the classroom in the eyes of the parent.
- Summarize what the speaker is saying after he has been speaking for a while.

Keys to Effective Classroom Management

- You will set the tone for conversations with parents. Before you can give advice that can be used by the parents, you need to understand their point of view.
- Building the relationship through active listening is critical to promoting the parents' involvement in their child's education both now and in the years to follow.

Using "I" Statements

The Issue

Adults tend to tell people what to do without recognizing that they are not in charge of the actions of the other party.

Overview

The use of "I" Statements promotes respect for the other person, recognizing that they are responsible for their actions. These statements allow you to express your feelings without causing the other person to become defensive.

Goal

◆ To learn to express concerns using "I" Statements. This conveys your concerns without judgment or expectation of results.

Solutions

An "I" Statement takes the form of "when you (action), I feel (descriptor)." Rather than a "You" Statement such as "You need to (action)", the "I" Statement tells only what I can control—my feelings. It does not tell the other person what to do. An example of an "I" Statement would be, "When you are late, I am worried" rather than the "You" Statement, "You need to be on time."

Determine whether or not the following examples are "I" Statements:

1. When you tell me about Shawn's behavior, I am worried about his safety.
2. When Callie is late for the program, I am concerned that she will be confused.
3. When Justin hits his sister, you need to discipline him immediately.
4. When Abby throws toys, I am worried that someone is going to get hurt.
5. When Brady gets in trouble at school, you need to take away his TV privileges.
6. When you spit on your friends, I feel angry because I know it upsets your friends.

Keys to Effective Classroom Management

◆ The "I" Statement takes the perspective of an equal, but the "You" Statement takes the point of view of a parent (telling the other person what to do). When working with families, talk with them as adults, not as the "wise parent" telling the child (the parent) what they have to do.

(Statements 3 and 5 above are not "I" Statements.)

Parent Conferences

The Issue

Parent conferences are an important part of the preschool experience. Through planning and good communication, parent conferences can be positive experiences for you and the parents who are supporting the children in their development.

Overview

When parents and teachers work together to meet children's educational and social needs, then the children, parents, teachers, and school benefit. It's a win-win situation!

Goal

◆ To meet successfully with parents to discuss the strengths and needs of their child

Solutions

Consider the following:
◆ Let the parents know about the parent conferences ahead of time in clear, non-threatening language.
◆ Let the parents know the purpose, place, and time of the meeting.
◆ Be willing to accommodate the parents' work schedules.
◆ Be aware that parents may be apprehensive about parent-teacher conferences, particularly as children reach school age.
◆ Make plans for the children's supervision during the conference.
◆ Choose a comfortable setting and ensure privacy.
◆ Use adult-size chairs and tables.
◆ Arrange the furniture so that you are not sitting behind a desk. The room arrangement should provide equality. If an outsider coming into the room can figure out where you will sit, it is not "equal."
◆ When possible, offer snacks and coffee or tea.
◆ Make a plan of what you want to talk about in the meeting.
◆ Take time to build rapport.
◆ Use language that parents will understand, not educational jargon.
◆ When sharing information, begin and end on a positive note.
◆ Summarize the discussion at the end of the meeting.
◆ Thank the parents for coming and sharing their suggestions.

Keys to Effective Classroom Management

◆ Remember that many families prefer frequent informal contacts as opposed to the occasional parent conference.
◆ Be sure to make parent contacts early in the school year—don't wait for behavior problems to surface before making the first contact. The time that you spend up-front in building a relationship with parents will pay off in the long run.

Telephone Conversations

The Issue

Telephone contacts are convenient and provide a source of frequent communication with parents. Most parents have telephones, and the cell phone has made communication even easier. If parents lack reading skills, the telephone provides an effective mode of communication.

Overview

Contacting parents by phone regularly is an effective way to work together to support the child.

Goal

- To have positive and beneficial telephone conversations that support the children's success in the classroom

Solutions

Consider the following:

- Never deliver negative information over the phone. Criticism over the phone is very difficult because there is no opportunity to observe nonverbal communication.
- Ask parents when it is convenient to call them.
- Don't call parents at work unless they are able to receive calls on the job.
- Let the parent know who is calling at the beginning of the call.
- Call the parent by name to personalize the call.
- Have a clear idea of your reason for calling.
- Stay on topic and keep the call relatively brief.
- Allow enough time for the parent to ask you questions.
- Let parents know when you can be contacted by phone.
- Thank the parent for his or her time before ending the call.

Keys to Effective Classroom Management

- There is a significant disadvantage in not being able to see the other person's nonverbal communication during a telephone conversation. For this reason, check your perceptions to make sure that you understand what the parent is saying.

Written Communication

The Issue

Exchanging information through written communication is often convenient because both parties can respond at the time they find most convenient. Some of the common forms of communication include e-mail, home-school notebooks, notes, classroom newsletters, classroom letters, and handouts.

Overview

Written communication provides a convenient way of exchanging information. This communication will support children's success in the classroom.

Goal

◆ To be an effective communicator of information to parents through written form

Solutions

Consider the following ways to exchange written communication:

E-mail

◆ Be aware of your school's policy on e-mail.
◆ Keep your written responses brief; otherwise e-mail becomes very time-consuming.
◆ Be aware of confidentiality issues with e-mail—it should not be open to inspection by others.
◆ Have a specific time of day that you regularly answer e-mail.
◆ Do not deliver criticism via e-mail.
◆ Be aware that e-mail has the disadvantage of being misinterpreted because there is no face-to-face contact.
◆ Be aware that e-mail leaves a paper trail of written communication.
◆ Think before responding. It is too easy to type a negative message and hit reply!

Home-School Notebook

◆ This is a notebook that goes from home to school in the child's backpack daily.
◆ It is best used with just a few children because it is time consuming.
◆ With children who do not or cannot speak, it is a good way of communicating with the parents.
◆ The parent regularly writes what is going on with the child in the notebook. You respond and inform the parent about what the child is involved with at school.
◆ You can write instructions for at-home, supportive activities for parents.

Notes

♦ Individual notes should not be used to deliver negative information.

♦ Individual notes are time-consuming so they should be brief and occasional.

♦ Thank-you notes are especially appropriate for parents who help with the classroom in any way.

♦ Attractive stationery or notepads appropriate for preschool are great for short notes to parents.

Newsletters

♦ Classroom newsletters are effective ways of communicating what the class is working on. When possible, enlist parents in helping with the newsletter. Appropriate features on a regular basis include birthdays, projects, pets, field trips, parent columns, parenting tips, stress-reduction methods, new toys in the classroom, and holiday news.

Classroom Letters

♦ This is a good way to deliver the same information to the parents of every child in the classroom.

♦ Some of the same information that would be part of a newsletter can be included in a classroom letter. The letter is quicker than the newsletter!

♦ The classroom letter is an excellent way to let parents know about class projects, especially when they need to send materials, refreshments, and other items.

♦ A monthly calendar with upcoming events posted can be printed on the back of the letter.

♦ When appropriate, include the children in drafting a letter to parents using chart paper in front of the classroom. The children can contribute to the letter as the teacher scribes on the chart paper.

Keys to Effective Classroom Management

♦ Watch your handwriting and spelling carefully. Parents expect teachers to have good spelling and handwriting skills. Use a word processor and spell check if these are not your strengths.

Extending Learning Into the Home

The Issue

Young children may learn a particular skill or concept at school, but this does not guarantee that it will be transferred into the home and community setting. Children also learn to be "situationally appropriate": they learn that a specific set of behaviors is expected in one situation, while another set of behaviors is expected somewhere else. When the expectations at home and school are similar, then children learn a consistent set of behaviors that will enable them to be more successful in those settings.

Overview

When parents and teachers work together to extend learning into the home, children are better able to transfer what they learned in school. This includes social skills, language skills, academic skills, and other learning.

Goal

◆ To work together with parents to ensure that children are able to extend the skills and concepts from school into the home and community

Solutions

Use the following ideas to encourage parents to extend what their child learns at school into the home:

◆ Establish home communication at the beginning of the school year or when the child is new in the classroom.

◆ Post the classroom rules and let the child and parents know what is expected.

◆ Have parent meetings where parents can visit as a group to learn about the classroom.

◆ There are many vehicles for extending learning that teachers can use:
  - Home-School Notebooks
  - Newsletters
  - Classroom Notes
  - Backpacks or boxes with materials and tasks for targeted concepts
  - E-mail and websites when families have web access
  - Classroom home page with extension activities when families have web access

◆ When suggesting activities or tasks that families can do at home, be specific:
  - What is the parent supposed to do?
  - What is the child supposed to do?
  - How often does it need to be done?
  - How long should they work on it?
  - What needs to be returned to the classroom?
  - When does any material need to be returned?

Keys to Effective Classroom Management

◆ Working to extend learning into the home on a regular basis is important. It should happen with all children, not just when a child is experiencing social or behavior problems.

Working With Parent Volunteers

The Issue

Some classrooms are fortunate enough to have parents who are able to volunteer their time and talents in the school or center.

Overview

Sometimes parents are expected to arrive at the classroom with the same knowledge of teaching as school staff. Some parent volunteers have strong "kid skills" and knowledge of learning, even without formal training. To utilize the talents and gifts that parent volunteers contribute, provide training regarding expectations in the classroom. When teachers provide orientation and training for volunteers, they are better able to meet the needs of the children, the classroom, the teacher, and the school.

Goal

◆ To support parent volunteers who make significant contributions to the learning and behavior of the children

Solutions

Consider the following:

◆ Always show an attitude of respect and kindness. Volunteers contribute their time by choice.

◆ You are in the leadership role and need to meet with volunteers before they assist in the classroom. When providing tips for instruction, you may need to meet prior to the beginning of the school day to explain the upcoming lessons and projects.

◆ Before volunteers enter the classroom, they need to be aware of confidentiality. What goes on in the classroom stays in the classroom. Talking about children, you, or the classroom with friends in the community is not appropriate and can do much damage.

◆ During the orientation session, discuss the program goals, policies, and procedures of the classroom.

◆ Show the volunteer where to find materials, how to set up activities, and how to use equipment.

◆ Explain classroom rules and your behavior management system. Behavior management can become an issue of disagreement between teachers and other adults.

◆ Create an atmosphere where the volunteer feels accepted and appreciated.

◆ Give volunteers a variety of tasks so that they have interesting and varied schedules.

◆ Be sure to provide feedback so that they know that you are aware of what they are doing.

◆ Be a positive role model.

◆ Recognize and reward volunteer service. School-wide functions and meetings where volunteers are recognized let them know that their contributions are appreciated.

Keys to Effective Classroom Management

◆ As a teacher working alone, you are not always able to meet the needs of every child. Classroom volunteers provide opportunities for meeting the needs of more children more effectively.

◆ Volunteers do not have to help out—they choose to do so. Let them know that they are valued members of the classroom community.

Dealing With Anger

The Issue

When you are frustrated with a child's behavior, the parents are often frustrated, as well. Because you are the one to confront the parent with the child's behavior, the parent may become angry with you. When teachers blame parents and parents blame teachers, it is the child who loses. Avoid placing blame and work together for the good of the child.

Overview

You need to be prepared to deal with anger. Teachers and parents need to work through the anger so that they can begin to problem solve effectively.

Goals

◆ To listen to parents and let them express their anger about the situation, then work together to problem solve for the benefit of the child

Solutions

Consider the following:

◆ Remember that parents often have legitimate reasons for being angry—schools and teachers do make mistakes and may not always recognize them. Many times there is a history of problems with schools or teachers that you may not know.

◆ Always be courteous.

◆ Listen—don't interrupt and insert your opinion.

◆ Don't argue or become defensive.

◆ If they talk louder, speak more softly.

◆ Pause and speak slowly before responding.

◆ Don't minimize the problem.

◆ Summarize and reflect their concern.

◆ Exhaust their complaints. Find out if there is anything else bothering them about the situation.

◆ Reflect the parents' feelings and beliefs back to them to let them know that you understand what they are saying.

◆ Ask open-ended questions such as, "How did this happen?"

◆ Avoid asking "why" questions. This leads to defensiveness for parents.

◆ When dealing with anger, your role is not to problem solve, but to communicate concern.

◆ The emphasis here is on building trust.

◆ Be aware that anger often does not result from one situation. It may be a build-up of situations over time that have upset the parents because the perceived lack of concern for their child and them.

◆ Parents should be able to express their anger, but you do not have to tolerate abuse. If anger becomes explosive or abusive, excuse yourself from the situation and contact the parents at a later time.

◆ Never allow a parent's anger to influence you to do things that you know are not in the child's best interest.

Keys to Effective Classroom Management

◆ Often the child is angry, you are angry, and the parents are angry, too. And, all three parties have very real and understandable reasons for the anger. Because the only emotions that people can control are their own, recognize your anger and talk with a trusted friend who will listen and provide insight.

Overprotective Families

The Issue

Some parents encourage independence and social behavior in their children, while other parents fear that their children will be hurt by others. These children may develop into fearful children themselves.

Overview

When families are overprotective, it can interfere with the child's ability to participate and learn in the school environment.

Goal

- To help parents gain confidence in children's ability to work more independently and confidently in the school setting

Solutions

Here are some ways to work with parents and children to promote self-esteem and independence.

- Recognize the fact that not all families value independence in children.
- Avoid labeling a family as "overprotective." Some cultures may value interdependence or strong family attachments.
- Recognize that overprotection on the part of parents may be a result of their experiences with living in a dangerous environment.
- Be aware that the child's health history may be a very real concern of parents, which may be perceived by teachers as overprotection.
- Build a relationship of trust with the family.
- Parent conferences help the parent to understand the school, and the school to understand the parents.
- Observe basic safety rules and inform parents of safety rules.
- Let the parents know about your expectations for independence.
- Encourage children to accomplish small tasks independently. Praise them for these accomplishments. Send home positive notes to parents about these tasks. Parents are pleased to know when their children do so well. However, make sure that you don't encourage children to do things that would be offensive to parents or perceived as dangerous.
- Build children's sense of confidence and competence. Gradually increase their responsibilities and independence in the classroom.
- School "performance" programs (holiday programs, singing, skits) often are helpful in allowing parents to see how well their children are able to participate with the other children in the school.
- Be aware that some parents of children with disabilities may tend to be very protective. As these children develop and mature, it may be difficult for parents to let go. However, many of these children often overcome their problems and are able to participate more fully in the classroom with their peers.

Keys to Effective Classroom Management

- Start small. Build on success. Praise the child for steps toward independence. Communicate the child's success to parents.
- Don't automatically assume that parents are overprotective if you do not understand their culture or the child's health history.

Dealing With Denial

The Issue

Some families do not recognize that a child has a significant behavior problem. They may rationalize the problem or excuse it.

Overview

To enlist the parents in helping to solve the problem, parents need to understand that the child needs to learn appropriate behaviors.

Goal

◆ To have parents become partners rather than adversaries in helping children learn appropriate social behavior

Solutions

Consider the following:

◆ Find time to communicate with parents on a regular basis.

◆ Make sure that you have communicated with parents before the problem behavior occurs. When your first call to a parent is about a behavior problem, it may not be accepted easily.

◆ Keep in mind that your criticism of a child may be taken personally by the parent.

◆ Never criticize the child personally—focus on the need to change the behavior, not the child.

◆ Avoid any statements that promote defensiveness such as:
  ◆ Why do you think she did that?
  ◆ Is there anything going on at home to make her act that way?
  ◆ Does she do this at home too?
  ◆ Do her brothers or sisters _____?
  ◆ Haven't you taught her not to _____?
  ◆ Are you giving her enough attention at home?

◆ When a parent has an explanation for the child's behavior, listen. Then work with the parents to teach the child a better way to get her needs met.

◆ Don't minimize the behavior problem or ignore it.

◆ Emphasize the need to teach a better way rather than punish or blame.

Keys to Effective Classroom Management

◆ Remember to look for the positive characteristics of the child. When teachers focus on deficits or needs, it may seem like they are "picking on" the child. Every child has strengths and gifts, and it is important to remember these when communicating with parents.

Dealing With Substance Abuse

The Issue

Children who come from families where alcohol or drugs are abused are seriously at risk for behavior problems. Children's needs for attention and nurturing are met inconsistently. They learn that they get what they need when daddy is "feeling good" or mommy is "happy." The rest of the time their needs are met only when they make demands, often through inappropriate behavior. Children may lack a basic sense of security and boundaries.

Overview

Recognize that substance abuse is prevalent in our society and cuts across all social and economic boundaries. It destroys the lives of parents and children, and it has a serious impact on children.

Goal

◆ To recognize that substance abuse in the family affects classroom behavior. Rather than blame parents, communicate with them regularly to let them know about the child's needs.

Solutions

Although it is hard not to blame parents when you see them failing to meet the child's emotional needs, recognize that addiction is a serious disease, similar to cancer or diabetes. Here are some ways to help:

◆ Educate yourself about addictions such as alcoholism through reading, workshops, or the Internet.

◆ Build a relationship with the family. Communicate your concern about the child.

◆ When the child has classroom behavior problems, contact the parent. Always focus on the child. Avoid statements that are accusing such as, "Is there anything going on at home that could cause this?" Express your concern about the child. Use I-Statements (see page 115).

◆ Be aware that a parent's concern for his or her child may be the motivating factor for that individual to seek help, which may be going to treatment, joining a support group such as Alcoholics Anonymous (AA), or leaving an addicted spouse.

◆ Encourage the school office or counselor (if available) to display informational materials for parents, including brochures on mental health and addiction, such as: helping with homework, the school curriculum, selecting toys and games, school personnel and services, your Parent-Teacher Organization, children's community mental health services, addiction: Where to go for help, and family support groups

◆ Help the children learn to express their feelings verbally.

◆ Have clear rules and boundaries in the classroom. Consistency is particularly important for a child who has an addicted parent.

◆ Be aware that child abuse must be reported. A child from a family with addiction problems is at risk for various types of child abuse. If you observe signs of child abuse you are required by law to report it to your local children's protective service office. This may also serve as a motivating factor for parents to get help for addiction.

Keys to Effective Classroom Management

◆ Addiction is a family disease. There are support groups for families and children such as Al-Anon and children's groups. When a parent gets help, the child's behavior may actually get worse because the upheaval in the family system is such a massive change and may be resisted by family members. Even when families get help for addiction, it is a painful process that will take time and persistence.

Family Empowerment

The Issue

Families need to learn skills to support their children as successful members of the school community during preschool and the years to come.

Overview

A familiar saying is that if you give a person a fish you have fed him for a day, but if you teach him to fish you have fed him for life. This adage has great relevance when working with families.

Goal

♦ To help families express their hopes and dreams for their children and to be active in all phases of the child's education—not just passive recipients of "whatever the school thinks best"

Solutions

Do:

♦ Provide information to parents on behavior management principles, particularly in regard to what works at school with the child

♦ Provide opportunities for families to collaborate with each other.

♦ Ask about family preferences.

♦ Assist families in considering what their needs are and what is most important for their child within the family context.

♦ Build a relationship of trust between the family and school.

♦ Let families know about workshops and training sessions that provide information on child development and family involvement.

♦ Brainstorm together to solve problems.

♦ Provide information on where the parent can get needed resources.

♦ Assume that parents are high-minded, well intended, and capable.

Don't:

♦ Assume the position of "professional distance."

♦ Think that you must have all the answers.

♦ Do for parents what they need to learn to do for themselves.

♦ Develop a "savior complex"—families have their own goals and you cannot impose your values on them or "fix" them.

♦ Try to solve everyone's problems.

Keys to Effective Classroom Management

♦ Empowerment can occur when families and professionals collaborate to increase families' desire to help their children, improve their knowledge and skill base, and take action to help their children.

Putting It Into Practice: Sandy

The principles supporting this narrative are:

◆ Classroom management requires teachers to deal with individual problems.

◆ When one technique fails, try another.

◆ Some children respond quickly, while others require a longer time to heal.

◆ Involve the family as much as possible when dealing a child's problems.

◆ Sharing personal experiences will facilitate children's understanding of their own problems.

◆ Children may need instruction about expressing their feelings before they can verbalize their needs and concerns.

◆ Professional assistance beyond the classroom is necessary on occasion.

◆ Patience and good humor are essential to success.

Mrs. Carlson knew that Sandy's mother was ill when the school year started, and she knew that the illness was terminal. When the winter break came, Sandy's mother died. Mrs. Carlson made the time to attend the wake as well as the funeral, and she visited with Sandy on both occasions. She wondered how Sandy would respond in the classroom when she returned to school in January.

Sandy was a three-year-old middle child in a family of three, and Sandy's father had taken care of the family as his wife was dying. He, too, confessed concern about Sandy's well-being, because he knew that young children have extreme fears about losing their mothers. His mother came to stay with the family during his wife's extended illness, and she was planning to stay for about six months into the new year. Every precaution was being taken to ease the family into life without their mother.

Mrs. Carlson greeted Sandy on the day she returned to school and shared a quiet moment with her about how glad she had been to see her during the holidays. "I know you miss your mother," she said, "But I'm here to talk to you when you feel like talking about her. I remember how sad I was when my mother died."

Within a few days, Sandy announced during Circle Time, "My mother died." Though her classmates did not seem to react to the comment, Mrs. Carlson responded by saying, "Yes, Sandy, she did. Do you want to talk about your mother?"

Sandy did not respond at the time, but later she came to Mrs. Carlson and talked about her grandmother being in the home. "Granny cooks for us now," said Sandy. "She likes to play cards with me." In the weeks following, Sandy would sit close to Mrs. Carlson and on occasion she would make comments about her mother. "My mother's favorite color was blue. My Granny likes blue, too."

Mrs. Carlson knew about death education, and she brought in a few books to share with Sandy about death. Judith Viorst's *The Tenth Good Thing About Barney* and Leo Buscaglia's *The Fall of Freddy the Leaf* were two she

(continued on the next page)

shared. She happily noted that Sandy did not seem to need the assistance of a professional counselor to deal with her death experience, but Mrs. Carlson had been prepared to share the name of an area counselor if she a recommendation had been needed.

Mrs. Carlson also shared her experiences with death with Sandy. "I was sad for a long time when my mother died," she reminisced. "I still miss her sometimes." Sandy responded to Mrs. Carlson's nurturing, and her sad disposition improved throughout the school year. Sandy needed time to grieve, but Mrs. Carlson's attentive care helped her through her time of crisis.

Individual Solutions

SECTION TWO

The second portion of this book deals specifically with children who have persistent behavior problems. When you have your classroom management solutions in place, such as those practices presented in Section 1, and children continue to exhibit problem behavior, then it is time to use the principles that are addressed here in Section 2. Chapter 7, *Analyzing Problem Behavior,* will help you to systematically understand the factors that impact children's behavior within the classroom. This chapter should be read in its entirety since behavior analysis is a step-wise process. Other chapters in this section can be effectively used as a stand-alone resource. You can search out those ideas that apply to the child in question and use those that are appropriate for your situation.

Chapter 8, *Teaching Alternative Behaviors,* describes how to design instruction to replace the challenging behavior that children demonstrate in the classroom. With the use of the "Fair Pair," you can discover which goals to target so that children's negative behavior is replaced with a more effective positive one. Instructional methods are presented for teaching social skills. Additionally, a number of preventive strategies are discussed. Chapter 8 provides teaching scripts for instructing children in the use of appropriate social behaviors. These scripts are suggested methods of teaching, but you do not need to follow them verbatim. Chapter 9, Communication Skills, contains scripts and specific methods for teaching children to better communicate their needs. Ways of teaching young children to identify and express their feelings also are presented in Chapter 9.

Preschool Classroom Management

Analyzing Problem Behavior

**Chapter
7**

The question "What do you do when...?" regarding problem behavior can be very difficult to answer. There are many factors that influence a child's behavior. Rarely is there one action that will solve a behavior problem and rarely is there a simple solution. In this day and age of miracle drugs and fast food, it sometimes seems that it should be possible to find a way to solve a behavior problem on the spot. Changing behavior takes time and careful analysis. This chapter presents the process of behavior analysis, which is best understood if considered in its entirety before analyzing a child's behavior.

Analyzing behavior problems requires observation over a period of several days. The behavior must be described precisely, stating when it occurs, how often it occurs, and the conditions that surround the behavior. In fact, children with challenging behavior often have a repertoire of behaviors that they use in different situations. To understand the behavior, it must be observed in the context where it is seen typically.

Preschool Classroom Management is based on the belief that problem behaviors do not occur randomly or without reason. Challenging behaviors serve a purpose for the child. Teachers must develop a hypothesis regarding the reason that the child acts as he does. With most challenging behavior, the child either gets something (attention, toys, activities) or avoids something (sitting, working, sharing, peers).

One purpose of analyzing behavior is to be able to predict when it is likely to occur, so you can develop a plan to pre-empt the behavior. Another purpose of analyzing the behavior is to determine a replacement behavior that will serve the same purpose for the child. What can he be taught to do instead? In this way the child is able to have his needs met through appropriate behavior. Adjusting the situation to prevent troubling behavior and teaching the child another way to meet his needs, develops long-term solutions to the problem. Behavior analysis is the key classroom management tool to accomplish this. This process takes time, effort, and perseverance—but it pays off in the long run.

Events in the Child's Life

The Issue

The daily stresses that occur in the child's home life have an impact on the child's behavior at school. There are many events that influence a child's behavior before the child ever enters the classroom. Examples include illness, lack of sleep, a fight with a sibling in the car, cruel words from a peer on the bus or van, a struggle with a parent over what shoes to wear, and parental bickering. Although these life events do not *cause* the behavior, they increase the probability that challenging behavior will occur.

Overview

The adage "to walk a mile in someone else's shoes" encourages understanding of others, in this case children. Rather than blame the child, consider the environment and see if there are events that are troubling for the child. You will want to work with the family and others in the child's life to develop an environment that is "child friendly."

Goal

- To analyze the environmental factors that "set the child up" for challenging behavior so you can work with the significant others in the child's life to soften the impact of those factors

Solutions

Talk with the child's parents. Focus on wanting what is best for the child rather than placing blame on the parent. Always begin the conversation with a positive statement of concern for the child and a desire to help him gain control of his behavior.

Some of the areas to discuss with the parent include:

- observations of any changes in the child's behavior
- the parent's insight regarding the problem
- any health factors that might be influencing the child
- medications that could have negative side effects
- whether the child is getting enough sleep
- interactions with siblings or peers that might be troubling the child
- changes at home that might impact the child's behavior

During the parent conference, brainstorm ways to help the child. Solicit the ideas of the parents because they know the child better than anyone else. Work together to help the child gain behavioral control in a more peaceful environment.

Keys to Effective Classroom Management

- Events outside the school can have a serious impact on the child in the classroom. Teachers want to reduce the negative impact of these events whenever possible. Sometimes it is not possible to change things. Parents quarrel; grandmothers die; divorces happen; parents are transferred. When teachers understand the life of the child they can be empathetic and can cushion the effect of these events in the child's life. In addition, when parents understand the effect that the home has on the child at school, they can work to structure the environment for the child and provide support during difficult times. Difficult times are not an excuse for negative behavior. While teachers recognize the child's need for love and understanding, equally important is a structured, predictable school environment that provides security for the child in a world that is often stormy.

Triggers

The Issue

Negative behaviors do not occur haphazardly or in a vacuum. There are triggers for challenging behaviors: those events or situations that immediately precede the behavior. If you can determine what "sets a child off" and triggers negative behavior, then you can make adjustments to prevent or diminish the behavior.

Overview

Although you cannot completely prevent challenging behavior from occurring, you can reduce its frequency. This makes the behavior easier to deal with when it does occur. Otherwise, you spend a good portion of the day "putting out fires."

Goal

◆ To analyze the events that happen just before a negative behavior occurs, which allows you to change the classroom environment so that it is a more peaceful place for children. By reducing the amount of time that the child is engaged in negative behavior, you can enhance his self-concept as a valued member of the learning community.

Solutions

The steps in analyzing the triggers for problematic behavior are:

1. Immediately after the behavior occurs, record what was going on in the classroom when the problem behavior occurred.
2. Note when and where the behavior occurred.
3. Note who was playing with the child when the behavior occurred.
4. Note where your were when the behavior occurred.
5. Do this until there is a list of five or more episodes of challenging behaviors.
6. Look for a pattern.
    ◆ Does the behavior occur at a regular time of the day?
    ◆ Does the behavior occur during a particular type of activity?
    ◆ Does the behavior occur when specific children are together?
    ◆ Does the behavior occur when an adult is nearby or when an adult is not looking?
7. Make classroom adjustments:
    ◆ If the behavior occurs when the child is tired or hungry, adjust the schedule for rest or snacks.
    ◆ If the behavior occurs during a specific activity, try increased supervision during the activity. Sometimes specific toys or activities may need to be removed for a short time or altogether.
    ◆ Some children are well behaved individually, but may interact negatively with specific peers. In this case, increased supervision of peers is needed, or children may need to be separated for a time.
    ◆ Often children have negative behaviors to gain attention of adults. In this case give the child plenty of positive attention before the negative behavior occurs. Catch them being good!
8. Think about the classroom day. Can you predict when the child's negative behavior will probably happen? If so, you are on your way to planning for prevention. If not, more observation is needed.

Keys to Effective Classroom Management

◆ An ounce of prevention is worth a pound of cure. You are more effective when you learn to pre-empt challenging behavior.
◆ Children learn best when they use appropriate social behavior.
◆ Classrooms are more peaceful communities when situations that trigger negative behavior are avoided.

133

Pinpointing the Behaviors

The Issue

When you clearly describe and understand children's behavior, you can develop a plan to teach children to get their needs met in a more appropriate way—and you can tell whether or not their plan is working when you see the problem behavior less often. But unless you describe the behavior clearly, you will not really know if the behavior is improving—or if you are just getting used to it!

Overview

Children improve their behavior one step at a time, and to improve it, you need to be very specific about what you are doing. You can't change everything all at once! The behavior needs to be described precisely so that you can target one specific behavior at a time. This will determine if the behavioral improvement plan is working.

Goals

◆ To develop a specific plan to teach children a better way to get their needs met, and be able to measure the results

Solutions

What exactly is the child doing that is problematic? Describe the behavior in terms that are *clear* and *observable*. Examples include:

Vague Descriptions	Clear and Observable Descriptions
aggressive	pushes peer to get the toys first
noncompliant	does not respond to verbal instruction
tantrum	throws self on floor, pounds fists, and screams
picks fights	hits peers
hyperactive	moves out of place during instructional times
short attention span	changes activity during instructional times

Try the following examples for practice. Describe each of the following using an observable behavior.

Vague Descriptions	Clear and Observable Descriptions
mean to others	
has his own agenda	
distractible	
bullies others	
keeps to himself	
"talks back" to the teacher	

Keys to Effective Classroom Management

◆ When describing behavior, use the following as a test: If someone else who did not know the child came into the classroom and saw this behavior as described, would he or she recognize it? The behavior should be described so precisely that a stranger would be able to come into the classroom and count the number of times it occurred during the day.

Consequences for the Behavior

The Issue

Children develop behavior patterns based on many individual reasons, including their temperament, genetic factors, health factors, family interactions, and their personal history. The one area where you have the strongest influence is the child's interaction in the classroom. Children's behavior changes based on what follows it—the consequences. Some consequences cause the behavior to increase or stay the same. Other consequences cause the behavior to decrease.

Overview

Educators and school personnel often refer to "consequences" as a punishment or a negative event. Consequences are not necessarily positive or negative: whether consequences cause the behavior to get worse, get better, or stay the same depends on the individual child. When you understand the pay-off of a child's behavior, you can determine the function of that behavior for the child.

Goal

◆ To examine the consequences for a behavior to determine if what you are doing is effective. When you determine that a strategy is ineffective, try another way.

Solutions

Observe the child during the times that the challenging behavior is likely to occur.

1. When the child demonstrates the behavior, what happens?
2. What do you do?
3. What do the child's peers do?
4. Describe each of these in observable terms: pinpoint behaviors!

Try this strategy. Describe a specific child's behavior in observable terms.

Question	Action
What happens after the behavior?	
What do you do?	
What do peers do?	

Keys to Effective Classroom Management

◆ Consequences for behavior are different from punishment. Whether the consequences are punishing or pleasurable depends on the child's personal characteristics and past experiences. At this point you only need to determine what happens immediately after the negative behavior. On the next pages will be descriptions of why behaviors are often not what they seem to be on the surface.

◆ Unless you take a "scientific" approach to behavior change, the behavior may continue, or increase over time.

The Pay-Off for the Child

The Issue

Children behave as they do to have their needs met. What you think of as a consequence of a behavior is very different from how children perceive the consequence of their behavior.

Overview

When you examine the behavior from the point of view of the child, you can see what the pay-off is for him. For example, when a child bothers peers during Circle Time, you may think that the child has reached his limit and excuse the child to go explore the classroom. For the child who wanted to avoid sitting in the circle, this may be a rewarding outcome. In effect, you are rewarding the child for bothering his peers by letting him have free play with toys of his choice. Another familiar example is when you reprimand a child. This gives the child plenty of attention from both peers and you. What you perceive as negative may be very positive for the child. Analyze behavior from the child's viewpoint, recognizing that behavior serves a purpose for him. This helps you develop a plan to teach the child to get his needs met in a more appropriate way.

Goal

◆ To examine the pay-off of the behavior for the child, so you can see the difference between what you think the consequences are for the behavior versus what the child experiences as a consequence from his point of view

Solutions

After the negative behavior occurs, ask the following questions:
◆ What did the child receive as a result of the behavior?
◆ Did the behavior result in some sort of pay-off for the child?
◆ Does the behavior result in the child getting something?
◆ Does the behavior result in the child avoiding something?
◆ What are the reasons that the child might continue with this behavior?

Try this with a specific child and a specific behavior. Describe a specific child's behavior in observable terms using the following chart:

Question	Possible Pay-Off
What happened after the behavior?	
What did the child gain as a result of the behavior?	
Does the behavior result in the child avoiding something?	
What are some reasons that the behavior might continue?	

Keys to Effective Classroom Management

◆ Negative behaviors that occur on a regular basis usually have some sort of pay-off for the child—that is, they help the child get his needs met. Problem behaviors typically occur to gain social or material pay-offs, or they allow the child to avoid some event that he finds unpleasant.

Some Common Child Needs

The Issue

Challenging behaviors do not occur randomly or without reason. When a child demonstrates negative behavior, it is usually to fill some need that is lacking. There are some very common needs that you should keep in mind as you analyze behavior.

Overview

If you can pinpoint the need, then you can design a plan to help the child have his needs met in more appropriate ways. This can be done by changing the classroom environment, changing how you respond to behaviors, and teaching the child a more acceptable behavior to have his needs met.

Goal

◆ To learn to recognize children's common needs that are associated with negative behaviors so you can respond to these behaviors in a way that makes the behaviors invalid and ineffective

Solutions

There are two basic types of pay-offs for behavior: to get something or to avoid something. Some common things that children receive for challenging behaviors are attention, sensory stimulation, control of the situation, activities they like, or toys or other items that they want. On the other hand, some of the things that children want to avoid are low-preference activities (sitting, difficult tasks, lengthy tasks), certain types of sensory stimulation, and physical pain.

Note the behaviors and a typical pay-off that actually promotes the negative behavior.

Example of Behavior	Pay-Offs That Get Something
◆ making sounds of burping and passing gas	◆ peers laugh and are entertained
◆ throwing blocks in the Block Center	◆ the teacher has a "talk" with the child
◆ grabbing truck from peer	◆ the child gets to play with a favorite toy
◆ saying "no" to all teacher requests	◆ the child gains control of the situation

Example of Behavior	Pay-Offs That Avoid Something
◆ throwing scissors during a difficult art project	◆ avoids a task not developmentally appropriate
◆ scratching peer who comes too close	◆ peer leaves him alone
◆ hitting self in the ear	◆ diverts the child's attention from pain
◆ getting up during Circle Time	◆ avoids activity that is too lengthy

Keys to Effective Classroom Management

◆ Problem behaviors occur to get something a child wants or to avoid something that he does not want. Often the consequences that you perceive as negative are actually rewarding to the child. Be aware that some consequences reward negative behavior because the child avoids a task that he did not want to do in the first place.

Attention-Seeking Behavior

The Issue

Children differ in their needs for attention. The child that is ignored often is so hungry for attention that he will do anything to get it. On the other hand, the child who is used to being the center of attention will do anything he can to maintain his place in the sunshine. Children who enter a group situation for the first time must adjust to sharing the attention of the adult with other children. When children's needs for attention are not met you can expect to see negative behaviors to gain the attention of either adults or peers.

Overview

When you recognize that the purpose of the child's problem behavior is to get attention, you can develop a plan of action. The plan will differ depending on whether the child's behavior is to get the adult's attention or to get their peers' attention. In any case, it is possible to teach the child a better way to meet his needs.

Goals

◆ To learn to determine when the child is behaving to get adult or peer attention so you can develop a plan of action, and to teach the child more appropriate ways to meet his needs, thus improving behavior

Solutions

The questions listed below will provide insight regarding the purpose of the child's behavior. If the answer is "yes" to any of the questions below, the negative behavior may serve the purpose of gaining your attention.

◆ Does the negative behavior occur more often in a large group than when the child is alone or with a few children?

◆ Does the negative behavior occur more often when you are not paying attention to the child?

◆ Does the negative behavior occur more often when the child wants you to spend time with him?

◆ Do you see the negative behavior more when you are very busy with other children or tasks in the classroom?

For children who wish to get peer attention, examine the following questions:

◆ Does the negative behavior occur more often when the child is left out of activities with peers?

◆ Does the child have trouble joining groups or interacting with other children?

◆ Does the child lack social communication skills for interacting with others?

◆ Does the child have difficulty understanding social cues or social situations?

Keys to Effective Classroom Management

◆ Many children behave in negative ways to get attention. Some children may have difficulty adjusting to the group environment at school. Children who lack social and/or communication skills are likely to behave inappropriately to get the attention of playmates. Also, what you perceive as negative attention, such as scolding or reprimands, may be seen as positive by the child. When children are used to getting attention only for negative behavior, this type of attention is expected and comfortable for the child.

Avoidance Behavior

The Issue

When tasks are not developmentally appropriate, children are likely to want to avoid them. There are other factors that influence avoidance behaviors as well. These factors include the individual interests of the child, the child's attention span, home expectations, your attitudes, and a host of other possibilities. One of the major benefits of preschool is the development of work habits that will be conducive to academic success in the school years. For this reason, it is important to teach children to work within a group setting for increasing periods of time.

Overview

When you examine avoidance behaviors from a developmental perspective, it is clear that most children learn this pattern of behavior during the early years. You can prevent future academic and behavior problems if you begin to work with the children when they are young.

Goal

◆ To learn to recognize when a child uses negative behavior to escape a task or situation so you can develop a plan that will invalidate the avoidance behavior and teach the child a better way of meeting his needs

Solutions

Does a child use negative behavior to get out of a task that he does not like? If you can answer "yes" to any of the questions listed below, then consider the possibility that the child is behaving negatively to avoid a task or situation.

◆ Does the negative behavior occur more often when the child is asked to do something he does not like?

◆ Does the negative behavior occur more often when the child is asked to do something that he does poorly?

◆ Does the negative behavior occur more often when the child is asked to do something for a relatively long period of time?

◆ Does the negative behavior occur more frequently during structured time (standing in line, circle, tedious in-seat activities) than during free play?

◆ Does the negative behavior occur more often when the child is asked to clean up?

◆ Does the negative behavior occur more often when the child is tired of the task at hand and there are more interesting materials elsewhere in the classroom?

Keys to Effective Classroom Management

◆ Children can be masterful at avoiding things that do not appeal to them. If they behave negatively and succeed in avoiding the task, they learn that negative behaviors work for them, so they may use the same behaviors next time. When you send a child to the "thinking chair" for behavior that has the purpose of avoiding a task, the child is getting his way! The next time he does not want to do something, he is likely to use the same negative behavior. This is an example where being consistent, using the "thinking chair" again and again, is likely to make the behavior worse and not better!

Need for Control

The Issue

As children develop, they want to control the events and people in their lives, but they have much to learn about control over themselves and others. Some children have a stronger need to control than others. For example, children who lack boundaries at home and are allowed to do as they please will likely expect to control the classroom as well. Or, children who have had no opportunities to influence their life or environment may develop oppositional behavior. The classroom that promotes age-appropriate participation in decision-making is a safe place where children can learn developmentally appropriate ways to participate in decisions that impact their daily interactions.

Overview

When you understand that children's negative behavior represents a need to have some control over their lives, you can plan ways that teach children developmentally appropriate decision-making and classroom participation.

Goal

◆ To learn to recognize behaviors that say, "I need to have more control over my life" so you can plan activities and appropriate choices within the classroom environment

Solutions

Children's negative behaviors communicate a desire for control if you answer "yes" to many of the following questions:

◆ Does the negative behavior occur more often when the child is asked to do something?
◆ Does the behavior seem to get worse as you become more direct or confrontational?
◆ If you say, "yes," does the child say, "no" and vice versa?
◆ Does the child argue with whatever opinion you express?
◆ Does the child seem to want to take the lead most of the time?
◆ Does the child insist that he is right even when it is obvious that he is not?
◆ Does the child insist on having his own way most of the time?
◆ Is the child persistent in refusals and arguments?

Keys to Effective Classroom Management

◆ While oppositional behavior and a need to control are common in young children, these characteristics need to be addressed early on during the preschool years. Later in this chapter there are a number of strategies for dealing with this behavior. Some of the keys to working with this issue include:
  ◆ providing choices,
  ◆ avoiding direct confrontations,
  ◆ keeping an even temper in the face of opposition, and
  ◆ maintaining a classroom with structure, opportunities for developmentally appropriate decision-making, and consistent boundaries for behavior.
◆ When children demonstrate an unusually strong need for control, remember that the children's behavior is "about them." Do not take it personally.

Sharing Toys and Equipment

The Issue

When children enter the preschool environment they must learn to share, to wait, and to become part of a group. Negative behaviors such as tantrums may occur when children want a toy that someone else is using or when they are asked to wait to go into centers. Often children with the most problematic behaviors are those who have language delays and who have not yet learned to "use their words" to get what they want. Providing an environment that promotes language development is important in helping children develop the ability to express their wants and needs otherwise.

Overview

When you recognize that negative behavior is related to children's inability to express their wants or needs, or to the difficulty with functioning as part of a social group, then you can plan activities to build language and social skills. You also must make sure that the children do not get the desired toy or other item when they throw a tantrum or use other challenging behavior. And if it does occur, you can make sure that it is not rewarded.

Goal

◆ To learn to recognize when problem behavior is related to a child's inability to delay gratification, share toys, or be part of a group so this behavior can be prevented

Solutions

If you answer "yes" to many of the following questions, children are using negative behaviors to communicate a desire for tangible items.

◆ Does the negative behavior occur more often when the child has been told that he cannot have a toy or other item?

◆ Does the negative behavior occur more often when the child is interacting with other children and must share toys?

◆ Does the negative behavior occur more often when the child has been asked to wait to use something or play with something?

◆ Does the negative behavior occur more often when the child is playing in centers with other children?

◆ Does the child lack the ability to express himself verbally?

◆ Does the child have a short attention span when he plays with toys or other items, changing quickly from one toy to the next?

Keys to Effective Classroom Management

◆ Preschool children are growing and developing. Presumably, as infants their needs were met quickly and their crying signaled that they were in need. As preschoolers they are learning a totally different way of responding: no longer will crying be rewarded when the child wants something. Instead, the child is expected to wait his turn, to share with others, and to use words to communicate his needs.

◆ Work with parents so they can learn to encourage their children to communicate verbally rather than through negative behavior.

Sensory Stimulation

The Issue

Preschool teachers are familiar with the five senses. However, there are two more senses—the sense of movement (vestibular sense) and the sense of body position (proprioception). The sense of movement enables us to maintain our position and balance in relation to gravity. The sense of body position is related to the sensation from the muscles and joints as individuals move. Each child and adult has different needs for the type and amount of sensory stimulation. When children do not get their needs for sensory stimulation met it may result in problem behaviors in the classroom. Conversely, children with special needs, particularly those with Attention Deficit Hyperactivity Disorder (ADHD) or Autism Spectrum Disorder (ASD), frequently have sensory problems that negatively impact their behavior.

Overview

When you learn to recognize that a challenging behavior reflects a need for sensory stimulation, then you can design experiences that meet the child's sensory needs. The child may need a "sensory diet" that provides the optimal amount and type of sensory stimulation to promote classroom adjustment.

Goal

◆ To determine when the child's behavior patterns reflect a need for increased or decreased sensory stimulation so you can meet the sensory needs of children and develop a more peaceful classroom

Solutions

If you answer "yes" to many of the following questions, there may be children whose negative behaviors reflect a need for sensory stimulation.

◆ Does the child have a need to touch everything in sight?
◆ Does the child chew or mouth objects, suck his thumb, or other similar actions?
◆ Does the child rock or demonstrate other repetitive movements?
◆ Does the child have a short attention span?
◆ Is the child distractible?
◆ Is the child constantly in motion?
◆ Does the child prefer highly flavored foods?
◆ Does the child have no sense of danger on the playground or classroom?
◆ Is the child impulsive?
◆ Does the child have difficulty calming down once he is excited?

Keys to Effective Classroom Management

◆ Developing children have a need for sensory experiences that must be met in order for them to adjust to the classroom environment. Classrooms that provide too little physical activity and exploration are difficult for preschoolers. Circle Times that extend for long periods of time result in behavior problems when children lack sensory stimulation.
◆ For children with special needs, or for those with suspected special needs, the advice of an occupational therapist is important in designing a program to meet the child's needs.

Sensory Avoidance

The Issue

Some children, particularly those with special needs, such as Attention Deficit Hyperactivity Disorder (ADHD) or Autism Spectrum Disorder (ASD), are bothered by sensory stimulation such as touch, sounds, smells, taste, or movements. Others seek sensation, but easily become over stimulated. Some of these children may seem to be traumatized by everyday sensory experiences that occur in the classroom. They may refuse to touch the playdough or other textures. Others may spend much of their day trying to avoid other children and tend to be "loners." You can better understand children when you realize that this is not simply noncompliance or immature behavior, but it is a physical difference.

Overview

When you understand a child's need to "go easy" with activities that are difficult because of sensory processing problems, you can provide a safe place in the classroom where the child can "regroup," as well as avoid activities that present too much sensory stimulation.

Goal

♦ To determine when a child's challenging behaviors are an attempt to avoid unwanted sensory stimulation so you can structure the environment to ensure that the child is comfortable and can tolerate the sensory stimulation in the classroom

Solutions

If you answer "yes" to many of the following questions, there may be children in the classroom whose negative behaviors constitute sensory avoidance.

♦ Does the child react negatively when peers get too close to his personal space?
♦ Does the child cover his ears in response to environmental noises that do not seem to bother other children?
♦ Is the child a picky eater, particularly with certain food textures?
♦ Does the child refuse to engage in messy activities such as playing with playdough or finger painting?
♦ Does the child engage in behaviors that are hurtful to himself such as eye poking, picking his skin, biting himself, or other similar behaviors?
♦ Does the child become unusually anxious when there is too much noise or a high level of activity?
♦ Is the child bothered by crowds or large group activities?
♦ Does the child react negatively to others touching him, bumping into him, or other physical contact?
♦ Is the child bothered by the textures of certain clothing, tags in clothing, or nylon thread in the seams of clothing?
♦ Is the child bothered by sudden movement?

Keys to Effective Classroom Management

♦ Each of us, adults and children alike, can become overstimulated. When this occurs, things that normally would not bother us can become quite upsetting. For children who cannot tolerate large amounts of sensory stimulation, you need to "cushion" the environment and modify activities so that they are not traumatized by events that provide too much stimulation too quickly. Consulting with an occupational therapist can provide insights and information that will enable you to make classroom accommodations for these children.

Interactions With Others

The Issue

All human beings need to feel a sense of belonging. Young children want to feel that they are part of the classroom interactions. Some young children do not know how to join in, how to enter an ongoing activity, or how to begin an interaction with others. Sometimes these children will physically push others, hit them with a toy, or use some other form of physical initiation when they want to play. These "starters" are fairly common with infants and toddlers, but during the preschool years children develop more standard forms of communication to initiate interactions with others.

Overview

Children need to be taught how to join a group and how to get started in play with their friends. They also need supervised play periods, when you prompt children to help them learn the appropriate way of beginning an interaction with their friends.

Goal

- To learn to recognize that aggressive behaviors (such as hitting or grabbing toys) may indicate a lack of social skills so you can help children learn appropriate social skills

Solutions

If you answer "yes" to many of the following questions, then the child's challenging behaviors likely communicate a desire to interact with others.

- Is the child extremely "physical" or rough-and-tumble in his interactions with playmates?
- Does the child push or hit when trying to get an interaction started?
- Is the child seen as "immature" as compared to his same-age peers?
- Is the child avoided by peers?
- Is the child seen as aggressive by other adults in the preschool?
- Has the child been slow in developing language?
- Is the child rough with toys and materials?

Keys to Effective Classroom Management

- Young children want to be part of the ongoing activities in the classroom, but sometimes they do not know how to get started. Most preschoolers are developmentally ready to use words to get started in play. This is a skill that children are often expected to learn through "discovery learning" in their environment. For the child who has not learned how to initiate play or join in, these skills need to be taught directly. Refer also to "How to Become Part of a Play Setting" on page 90.

Difficult Times

The Issue

You know if you are a "morning person" or a "night person" and it is likely that you have times of the day that are more difficult to handle than others. During difficult times, one tends to have less patience, and sometimes even diminished ability to accomplish tasks, as compared to optimal times. Children, too, have times of the day that are more difficult for them. This phenomenon is often related to need for food or sleep. As adults, some of us are more adaptable to changes or lack of food or sleep than others. The same is true of children. Some children can tolerate being hungry or tired without significant behavior problems while other cannot.

Overview

When you recognize that specific times of the day are more difficult for certain children, you can make accommodations in the schedule and expectations for these children. This knowledge will enable you to prevent much inappropriate classroom behavior.

Goal

◆ To keep a behavior log so that you can see when problem behaviors are most likely to occur

Solutions

Using the chart on the next page, keep a list of when the behavior occurs for the children in the classroom who have the most problematic behaviors. Place a check under the child's name each time that there is a behavior problem. Then record the ongoing activity and whether the child was hungry or tired.

Keys to Effective Classroom Management

◆ Some children have times that are more difficult on a regular basis. When you keep this record over several days (or record in a different color of pen), then you can anticipate when the child is likely to have problems. This information enables you to prevent behavior problems by increasing supervision and modifying the schedule when possible.

Behavior Log

Time	Child 1 (initials)	Child 2 (initials)	Ongoing Activity	Hungry?	Tired?	Other?
8-8:30						
8:30-9						
9-9:30						
9:30-10						
10-10:30						
10:30-11						
11-11:30						
11:30-12						
12-12:30						
12:30-1						
1-1:30						
1:30-2						
2-2:30						
2:30-3						
3-3:30						
3:30-4						
4-4:30						
4:30-5						
5-5:30						

Difficult Transitions

The Issue

Most people have some difficulty with change. Young children, in particular, may have problems with changes in activities or routines. Children are creatures of habit, and changes in their schedules may throw them off. When you know about upcoming changes, it gives you time to prepare children and lessen any problems. Children also have little sense of time. They are used to working and playing on their own schedules. When they enter preschool they are expected to move with the group. It will help children if you provide cues prior to changes in activities to alert the child to the activity change.

Overview

Young children have a limited life experience. Much of their sense of security comes from having a predictable routine in their lives. You can provide both routine and cues to changes in the routine for young children.

Goal

◆ To provide predictable routines with cues to changes in routines and activities to enable children to handle transitions without tears or tantrums

Solutions

Suggestions for providing predictable routines so children can easily transition from one time of the day to another include:

◆ Develop a predictable schedule and routine for the classroom.

◆ Provide pictures that show the schedule and activities.

◆ Go over the schedule for the day at the beginning of the day, using the pictures of the activities.

◆ As activities are started and completed, refer to the pictures. Move the pictures from one location to the next as activities are completed.

◆ When there is going to be a change of activities, place a piece of paper with a question mark (sometimes referred to as a "wild card") to show that there will be a different activity that day.

◆ When changing from one activity to the next, sing a transition song, such as "The Clean-Up Song" or "Now It's Time to ____" (sung to the tune of "Here We Go 'Round the Mulberry Bush.")

◆ Give the children time to adjust to the change in activity. Don't expect them to snap into place like little soldiers. Refer to "Planning for Transitions" on page 61 for additional transition ideas and activities.

Keys to Effective Classroom Management

◆ Young children are used to being on their own timetable. Many of them are accustomed to eating on demand, playing when they are interested, and sleeping when they are tired. As children enter preschool, they learn to work and play with the group. Adjusting to this new experience can be improved by providing a predictable routine that provides security for children.

◆ Keep in mind that transitions from a preferred activity to a non-preferred activity are likely to result in problem behaviors. Changes require preparation and time for adaptation. When you understand this, you are able to support young children in adapting to the preschool setting. You also need to provide cues about changes in routine as well as changes in activities.

Difficult Situations, Places, and Things

The Issue

Human beings know where they are the most comfortable and least comfortable, or even miserable. Some places may be too noisy, others may be too boring, and still other places may be overstimulating. You need to recognize that some places may be difficult for a particular child, and this discomfort may predict problem behavior. Also, certain activities and situations may be linked to behavior problems. Two children who may be fine individually can have serious behavior problems when they are together. And some children may have behavior problems during specific types of activities.

Overview

When you can predict the places where problem behaviors are likely to occur, then you are able to redirect or prevent challenging behaviors. You can do this by providing additional supervision, redirecting children before they get into trouble, reminding them of appropriate behavior, and making changes in the environment.

Goal

◆ To determine where problem behaviors occur through observing and recording so you can design a plan to prevent the behavior from occurring

Solutions

Using the Problem Behavior Chart on the next page, observe the child for at least three days to determine where the problem behavior occurs. Record the specific challenging behavior. Make sure to pinpoint the behavior specifically (as discussed on page 134), and then record where the behavior occurred under "Place." Fill out the next column by recording objects or toys that the child was playing with or using when the behavior problem occurred. Under "Specific Persons" record the name of the child that the child under consideration was interacting with when he or she demonstrated the behavior. Finally, place a check in the last columns if you think that the child experienced too much or too little stimulation during the incident.

Keys to Effective Classroom Management

◆ In analyzing the problem behavior, there are many influences that need to be considered. This recording process will enable you to consider whether certain places in the classroom were difficult for the child, whether it was a "difficult combination" of children, or whether specific toys or objects were associated with the behavior. When the child experiences a difficult place, he or she needs closer supervision there, additional preparation prior to going there, instruction in appropriate social behavior for that place, and a great deal of understanding. When there is a "difficult combination" of children, you can either separate the children for a time, or you can provide more supervision and instruction in appropriate behavior when they are together. With difficult objects, the toys can be put away for a while, and then when they are reintroduced, you can remind the child how the toys are to be used.

Problem Behavior Chart

Name: _____

Specific behavior	Place	Objects or toys	Specific persons	Too much stimulation?	Too little stimulation?

Problem Behavior Questionnaire

The Issue

An accurate understanding of a child's behavior is critical to developing a plan to teach the child a better way to get his needs met.

Overview

When you understand the factors that impact a child and his behavior, then you are able to design effective interventions that prevent the behavior from occurring (or occurring less often). And you can teach the child a better way to get his needs met.

Goal

◆   To answer questions on the questionnaire, so you can develop a more complete picture of the factors that are influencing the child

Solutions

Complete the Problem Behavior Questionnaire on the following page to understand a child's specific behavior.

Keys to Effective Classroom Management

◆   Behavior does not occur in a vacuum. It occurs because it meets the needs of the child, or because it has helped the child to get his needs met in the past. It is better to analyze the behavior and teach the child an appropriate way to behave, rather than simply punish for behaviors that have worked for him in the past.

Problem Behavior Questionnaire

Name _____ Date _____

Specify one problem behavior _____

Question	Answer
1. What home factors may be influencing the behavior?	
2. What happened earlier in the day that could influence the behavior?	
3. What is happening in the classroom when the behavior occurs?	
4. Who is the child interacting with when the behavior occurs?	
5. What times of day are usually problematic?	
6. Where does the behavior occur?	
7. Does the behavior occur when the child is bored?	
8. Does the behavior occur when the child is not directly supervised?	
9. Does the behavior occur when the child is with a specific child?	
10. Does the behavior occur when the child is overstimulated?	
11. Does the behavior occur when the child has been told "no"?	
12. Does the behavior occur when you are busy with other children?	
13. Does the behavior occur to get your attention?	
14. Does the behavior occur to get peer attention?	
15. Does the behavior occur to get toys or activities that the child wants?	
16. Does the behavior occur to avoid cleaning up?	
17. Does the behavior occur during changes of activities?	
18. Does the behavior occur during changes in the regular routine?	
19. Does the behavior occur to avoid something the child does not like?	
20. Does the behavior occur to help the child calm down?	

Classroom Behavior Chart

The Issue

When a child displays a problem behavior, it is important to determine how often negative behaviors occur.

Overview

By completing the Classroom Behavior Chart on the following page, you will gather a record of the actual occurrence of the behavior. This procedure can be used when analyzing a behavior, as well as later to see if the behavior is improving. A completed chart provides a record of the behavior so that a behavior change plan can be developed. This record can be completed again after the behavior change plan is in place.

Goal

◆ To keep a record of the problem behavior for one child

Solutions

Complete the form on the following page. Each time that the behavior occurs place a tally mark beside the time interval. If the behavior lasts longer than a minute, record how long it lasted. The suspected "Trigger" and "Consequence/Pay-Off" can also be recorded.

Keys to Effective Classroom Management

◆ Your perception may be that a negative behavior occurs "all the time." When you use this behavior chart it will tell how often the negative behaviors actually do occur. Also, you may think that a consequence such as the "thinking chair" is working when it is in fact **not working at all**. When you use a behavior chart such as this one, you can tell if the behavior is actually improving.

Classroom Behavior Chart

Name _____

Specify **one** problem behavior _____

Time	Behavior	Tally	Time	Trigger	Consequence/ Pay-Off
6:00-6:30					
6:30-7:00					
7:00-7:30					
7:30-8:00					
8:00-8:30					
8:30-9:00					
9:00-9:30					
9:30-10:00					
10:00-10:30					
10:30-11:00					
11:00-11:30					
11:30-12:00					
12:00-12:30					
12:30-1:00					
1:00-1:30					
1:30-2:00					
2:00-2:30					
2:30-3:00					
3:00-3:30					
3:30-4:00					
4:00-4:30					
4:30-5:00					
5:00-5:30					
5:30-6:00					

Putting It Into Practice: Brenda

The principles supporting this narrative are:

- Classroom management requires teachers to deal with individual problems.
- When one technique fails, try another.
- Some children respond quickly, while others require a longer time to respond.
- Involve the family as much as possible when dealing with a child's problems.
- Sharing personal experiences will facilitate children's understanding of their own problems.
- Children may need instruction about expressing their feelings before they can verbalize their needs and concerns.
- Professional assistance beyond the classroom is necessary on occasion.
- Patience and good humor are essential to success.

Brenda began biting soon after she joined Mrs. Sprott's class in the fall of the year. Four-year-olds usually don't bite, but as Brenda's teacher investigated the family situation, she began to understand why Brenda was biting. Initially, Brenda's parents were concerned, and they were at a loss to explain the behavior. As Mrs. Sprott held conferences with Brenda's parents she was able to identify variables that might be the source of Brenda's aggressiveness.

Brenda was adopted at six months as an only child into a family of older parents who both work. After school, she stayed in a relative's home where several older children resided. All of the children, including the girls, were rowdy and roughhoused regularly. Brenda's defense against the older children was to bite and fight for protection. When she came to school, she resorted to biting behavior, because biting was a familiar practice for her. Mrs. Sprott began to believe that the aggressive older children and the lack of positive interactions with other children her age led to Brenda's biting.

At first, her biting was minimal, and most children were able to assert themselves to avoid Brenda's teeth. But as the weeks progressed, several children became her favorite targets; and Mrs. Sprott observed that they were children that Brenda appeared to like quite well. Despite taking her aside to talk about the dangers of biting, as the year continued, it appeared that Brenda's biting was worsening. Mrs. Sprott began an active campaign to watch Brenda closely to help her avoid her negative biting activity.

But Brenda continued to bite. Helping children understand prosocial interactions is the responsibility of any teacher of young children, but talking to Brenda about losing friends or helping her recognize how she had hurt her friends with her bites did not have much impact on her. The children who were assertive avoided Brenda's bites; the other children were easy targets each and every day.

The next step Mrs. Sprott planned was to intervene before Brenda's biting behavior began each morning. At Brenda's arrival, Mrs. Sprott would greet her, take her aside, and talk to her about refraining from biting. "Say to yourself," Mrs. Sprott instructed, "Don't bite, don't bite." Then she asked Brenda to repeat the phrase, which she was able to do effectively. For most of the morning, this technique worked well, and Brenda seemed to be

progressing toward a goal of controlling herself. By 11:00 a.m., though, the self-talk technique would wear thin, and Mrs. Sprott noticed that Brenda would resort to biting, especially as lunchtime drew near.

Mrs. Sprott was patient, and she continued weekly discussions with Brenda's parents. One morning, when classroom activities were hectic, Mrs. Sprott decided that stronger measures were needed when Brenda bit three children in a 30-minute timeframe. She asked Brenda's parents to come again for another conference. This is the plan they agreed upon:

◆ Brenda would begin weekly play therapy sessions with the school counselor.

◆ When Brenda would bite a child, one of her parents would come pick her up from school and take her home, explaining that she had lost the privilege of being at school because of her biting. Because Brenda loved school so much, the plan of removing her from school was significant and made its point well.

Within weeks, Brenda's behavior improved. Her biting disappeared almost completely, although she would regress when a substitute teacher was in the classroom or if the school routine was disrupted. Mrs. Sprott was pleased when she recognized that Brenda's biting had disappeared by the end of the school year. The next year, her kindergarten teacher reported that she never observed Brenda biting at any time during her classroom experience in kindergarten.

Teaching Alternative Behaviors

Chapter 8

If negative behavior has worked for children in the past, then they are likely to use it again unless you can prompt and encourage them to use newly learned prosocial behavior. However, the new behavior that you expect children to use needs to be just as quick and effective as the old behavior. Sometimes children have appropriate social skills, but they use them inconsistently. Other children know how to behave appropriately but still use challenging behavior. This is not a social skill problem per se, but a "performance problem." In this case, you need to prompt children to use appropriate social skills that work in the classroom. When children do not use the appropriate the social skills in their repertoire, it is generally because their challenging behavior works more effectively.

This chapter assumes that challenging behavior is a need for instruction in social skills. While you would never consider disciplining a child for counting incorrectly, children are often disciplined for their lack of social behaviors that they do not know and have never been taught. This chapter presents lessons and methods to teach children appropriate social behaviors. The assumption is that if children learn a better way to have their needs met, then they will not need to use challenging behaviors.

Understanding the Problem

The Issue

The previous chapter presented suggestions for analyzing problem behaviors. Before designing a plan to address problem behavior, it is important to understand the behavior to prevent it from occurring—and to teach children a better way to get their needs met.

Overview

If you do not teach children a better way to get their needs met, then they are likely to continue with the problem behavior.

Goals

- To develop a scientific understanding of the problem behavior and to develop a plan that is based on proven principles
- To teach the child a better way to get her needs met so that she becomes a positive, contributing member of the classroom community

Solutions

The following are the 5 W's of problem behavior:

- WHO: Who are the people that the behavior is likely to occur with?
- WHAT: Exactly what is the child doing that is a problem?
- WHEN: When does the problem behavior occur and how often?
- WHERE: Where does the problem behavior occur?
- WHY: Why does the child behave as she does? What is the pay-off for the behavior?

After you answer these questions, you will be better able to design a plan that minimizes the behavior—and a plan to teach an alternative behavior.

Keys to Effective Classroom Management

- The answer to "What should I do when _____?" is not a simple, one-line answer. You will need to develop a clear understanding of the 5 W's of behavior so that you can design a long-term plan to change behavior. Behavior change takes time and effort.

Fair-Pair Rule

The Issue

For every inappropriate behavior, there is an alternative appropriate behavior. When you understand the purpose or pay-off of the negative behavior, you can develop a plan to teach the child an alternative appropriate action. For example, if a child grabs another child's hair when she wants him to look at her, the child needs to learn another behavior that serves the same purpose, such as teaching her to call his name, or if she lacks verbal skills, to gently tap him on the arm.

Overview

It is critical to teach children positive ways to get their needs met. If you simply try to stop a behavior that meets children's needs, then children may stop the behavior, but substitute a worse behavior.

Goal

◆ To determine an alternative behavior (fair pair) to teach children after their behavior is successfully analyzed

Solutions

Consider the following steps to analyzing inappropriate behavior:

1. Describe the inappropriate behavior to be addressed.
2. What is the pay-off for the behavior?
3. Think of an alternative behavior that you can teach the child. This is the "fair-pair" behavior.

The chart on the next page has several fair-pair behaviors listed. After you have read the examples, complete the others on your own.

Behavior	Pay-Off	Fair-Pair Behavior
Tantrum—kicks, screams	Gets toy she wants	Accepts "no" for an answer
Tantrum—kicks, screams	Gets toy she wants	Learns how to ask for a toy
Tantrum—kicks, screams	Avoids picking up toys	Picks up toys
Tantrum—kicks, screams	Gets out of circle	Sits in circle for five minutes
Hits peers	Gets peer's attention	
Hits peers	Gets toy from peer	
Hits peers	Avoids boredom of standing in line	

◆ The chart demonstrates that behaviors may *look* the same on the outside, yet be used for totally different purposes. Even when behaviors have the same purpose and pay-off, they may have totally different "fair-pair" behaviors, depending on the abilities and needs of the child. In the chart, the first two behaviors are tantrums with the pay-off of getting a toy. The second child needs to "learn to ask for a toy." For the first child the fair-pair behavior is "accepts 'no' for an answer." The first child already knows how to ask, but has problems with accepting "no." The second child has not yet learned to use words to get her needs met.

Keys to Effective Classroom Management

◆ What you decide to target as the "fair-pair" behavior depends on both the pay-off and the characteristics of the individual child. You should consider the child and ask, "What does the child need to learn, and how can I teach it to her?"

Alternative Ways of Communicating

The Issue

When you develop an understanding of problem behavior, you will learn that the behavior communicates a specific need. As the child grows, she learns to communicate her needs in more socially acceptable ways.

Overview

When you teach alternative behaviors, then you are teaching children more appropriate ways of communicating their needs.

Goal

♦   To teach children to express themselves verbally

Solutions

Questions to consider when teaching children alternative ways of communicating are:

♦   What is the specific problem behavior?

♦   What does the behavior communicate?

♦   If the child could say this in words, what would she say?

♦   What is the "fair-pair" behavior?

♦   What can you teach her to say instead?

♦   When does she need to use this alternative way of communicating?

♦   Where does she need to use this alternative way of communicating?

♦   With what other people does she need to use this alternative way of communicating?

Keys to Effective Classroom Management

♦   Much of social behavior communicates our needs. Many social skills are communication skills, both verbal and nonverbal. The following pages provide insights and specific examples of how to teach children better ways of communicating their needs.

Alternative Social Skills

The Issue

Not all environments promote behaviors that are socially acceptable at school, and not all children are able to tune in to the social expectations of the environment. This points to the need for direct instruction in the appropriate behavior in the school setting. The earlier this type of instruction begins, the better.

Overview

Social behaviors often are the determining factors of what makes people successful or unsuccessful in life. Children need to learn appropriate social behaviors at home and school through direct and incidental learning.

Goals

◆ To instruct children in social skills at a young age, so that they will improve their ability to get along in the preschool setting

◆ To set the stage for children's success during the preschool years and beyond

Solutions

Consider the following:

◆ When you see a behavior problem, consider it a need for instruction, not an action to be punished. Look at negative social behavior as a need for instruction.

◆ When you see a negative behavior, work to change the behavior and not blame the child.

◆ With children who demonstrate negative behavior, try not to take the behavior personally. The children are behaving in the way that has met their needs in the past. They must be taught a better way.

Keys to Effective Classroom Management

◆ When you work with young children, you are building a foundation for lifelong learning. Be aware that the social behaviors that you teach will be used for years to come.

◆ Be aware of your own behavior and model appropriate social behavior, which will be imitated by many children. If you yell or punish in anger, children see this and act accordingly. When you are calm and rational in times of stress, children react to and imitate these behaviors as well.

Social Scripts: General Principles

The Issue

After determining the social skills that children need to learn, be very specific about what you are going to teach. Most children learn social skills by observing others in their environment. Some communities model and reinforce aggressive behaviors that may be acceptable in the environment, but are not appropriate at school. If these children are not taught the social behaviors that are needed at school, they will continue the cycle of problem behavior in the school setting.

Overview

When you identify the social skills that children need to learn, you are better able to develop a teaching strategy to teach the specific social skills. By teaching children to behave appropriately, you are improving their existing social skills and building for future success in the school years.

Goal

◆ To understand the general principles of teaching social skills so that you can develop ways of teaching a "fair-pair" behavior for problem behaviors that arise in the preschool setting

Solutions

Use the following steps to determine what a "fair-pair" behavior might be:

1. **Ask, "What can I teach the child to do instead?"**
2. **Take the fair-pair behavior and break it down into three or fewer steps.** For example, if the child throws materials when frustrated, then suggest another behavior for the child when frustrated. The fair-pair behavior might be to:
   a. Take a deep breath.
   b. Cross your arms.
   c. Say to yourself, "Stay calm."
3. **Develop a social skills script using the following steps to teach the behavior:**
   a. Describe the social skill with the reason for it. For example, say to the child, "When you get frustrated, sometimes you throw things. When you throw things, someone can get hurt. What you can do instead is to take a deep breath, cross your arms, and say to yourself, 'Stay calm.'"
   b. Ask the child to describe the steps of what she needs to do when she is frustrated. For example, the child says, "I take a deep breath, cross my arms, and say to myself, 'Stay calm.'"
   c. Model this for the child.
   d. The next time the situation occurs, provide an example by saying, "I take a deep breath, cross my arms, and say, 'Stay calm.'"
   e. The child demonstrates the changed behavior.
4. **Think of ways that you can cue the child to use the behavior in the classroom. Provide the child with plenty of classroom practice.**
5. **Acknowledge the child for using the skill.**
6. **Enlist the family in reinforcing the behavior.**

Keys to Effective Classroom Management

◆ Keep it simple! Break down the positive behavior into three or fewer steps if children are going to be able to apply it in the actual setting.

◆ If you are unsure of what social behaviors to teach a child, look at what successful children do in the same situation. Then analyze the behavior of the socially successful child so that you can develop a social script for the child who is having social problems in the classroom.

Sample Script: Getting Started in Play

The Issue

If children are aggressive when they try to interact with their peers, they need to learn more appropriate social skills. If you want children to treat others with respect and consideration, teach them how to get started in their play with other children.

Overview

Developmentally, young children move from solitary play toward cooperative play. Most children learn how to initiate play with other children through observing their friends. Some children, however, do not know how to get started and may try to initiate play by pushing or grabbing others. As children mature, they need to learn more socially appropriate ways to approach others in their play.

Goal

◆ To teach children that they can join in the play using non-physical means, so that they will learn to do this rather than hit or push

Solutions

There are a number of appropriate ways to get started in play, depending on the situation, the language level of the child, the age of the child, and what is considered appropriate in the child's culture. Some cultures or groups are more accepting of physical contact than others. The script on the following page uses the method of teaching the child to join in by giving her friend a toy and saying, "Let's play."

1. **Describe the social skill.**

   "When you want to play with your friend, hand him a toy and say, 'Let's play.'"

2. **Have the child describe the social skill.**

   Ask the child, "What do you do when you want to play with your friends?"

   Child repeats what you told her.

   Say, "Right, I hand him a toy and say, 'Let's play.'"

3. **Model the behavior with the child.**

   "Watch me. I am going to show you how to ask your friend to play."

   Have the child tell if you asked your friend.

   Ask, "Did I ask my friend to play?"

   Child answers, "Yes."

   Say, "Right! I handed you the toy and said 'Let's play.'"

4. **The child models the behavior with you.**

   Say, "Show me how you ask your friend to play."

   Child models with you.

   Say, "Good, you handed me the toy and said, 'Let's play.'"

5. **Give an example of the social skill by modeling it with another child.**

   Ask, "What did I do?"

   The child states what you did.

6. **The child demonstrates with peer.**

   Say, "Show me how to ask Jessica to play."

   (Child demonstrates with peer.)

   Say, "Great! You gave Jessica the toy and said, 'Let's play.'"

Keys to Effective Classroom Management

◆ By planning to transfer the learning, the child is able to practice the social skills. You may need to cue the child about when to use the social skill, and you may need to involve the parents in helping the child practice the social skill. This will help the child to transfer learning to other people and situations.

◆ Transfer of learning:

   ◆ Cue the child to use the social skill before it is needed in the classroom. Right before the time when the social skill will need to be used, tell the child to remind her to hand her friend a toy and say, "Let's play."

   ◆ Send a note home to parents (see sample on the next page) explaining the social skill that you are teaching the children.

Dear Parents:

This week your child is working on the social skill of asking friends to play. If you can remind your child to use this skill at home it will help us at school.

This is what your child is learning:

1. When your child asks his or her friends to play, he or she hands them a toy.

2. Then your child says, "Let's play."

3. Your child does not push or hit friends when he or she wants to play.

Please acknowledge your child's positive behavior when he or she asks friends to play.

Thanks so much!

Sincerely,

_____

Sample Script: Taking Turns

The Issue

Children may need to be taught how to take turns. When they take turns successfully, reward this behavior when it occurs.

Overview

Young children may not have developed the ability to engage in taking turns. Toddlers start to practice this behavior when they hand you a toy, you comment on the exchange, and then give it back to them. If this "social reciprocity" is not reinforced or if it was never developed, then children may need to be taught to take turns.

Goal

◆ To teach children simple turn-taking, at first with small toys and one peer, and later with several peers and a variety of objects.

Solutions

The steps for teaching children to take turns are:

1. **Describe the social skill.**

   Say, "When you play with your friends, you need to take turns. You can say to yourself, 'My turn—your turn.'"

2. **Have the child describe the social skill.**

   Ask the child, "What do you do when you take turns?"

   Child says, "I say, 'My turn—your turn.'"

   Say, "Right, I say, 'My turn—your turn.'"

3. **Teacher models taking turns with the child.**

   "Watch me: I am going to show you how to take turns with the car." Roll a car and say, "My turn." Then give the child the toy car and say, "Your turn." After the child rolls the car, hold out your hand and say, "My turn." Repeat the process several times until the child is taking turns willingly. In this way, the child becomes secure in the fact that she will get to have a turn.

4. **The child models taking turns with you.**

   "Show me how you take turns."

   Child models taking turns with you, saying, "My turn—your turn" and taking turns with the car.

   Acknowledge the child's effort in taking turns.

5. **Give examples of the social skill by modeling it with a peer and asking the child if you shared with the peer.**

   "Watch me and tell me if I took turns with Jamie." Say, "My turn—your turn" and take turns using the car with Jamie.

   Then ask the child, "What did I do?"

   The child states what you did.

6. **The child demonstrates the social skill with a peer.**

   Say to the child, "Show me how to take turns with Jamie."

   (Child demonstrates with peer.)

   Say, "Great! You said 'My turn—your turn' and you took turns with Jamie."

Keys to Effective Classroom Management

◆ Turn-taking is a difficult concept for young children. When teaching a child to take turns, select toys that can be used briefly and then given to another child. Examples of objects that can be used in teaching children to take turns are toy cars, placing blocks on a structure, cooperative painting or drawing, or rolling a ball. Objects that require elaborate or imaginative play are more difficult because they require a longer time before the child would be expected to take turns. Also, new toys or toys that are treasured by the child are very difficult to use to introduce the concept of taking turns.

◆ Transfer of learning:

- ◆ Cue the child to take turns just before the situation occurs. Right before it will be used, tell the child to remember to take turns.

- ◆ Practice taking turns with a variety of objects.

- ◆ After the child is able to take turns with you and a peer, you can introduce the concept of "My turn—your turn—Jamie's turn."

- ◆ Send a note home to parents (see sample below) explaining the social skill that you are working on.

Sample Note to Parents

Dear Parents:

This week your child is working on the social skill of taking turns. Please remind your child to take turns at home to support what we are teaching at school!

This is what your child is learning:

1. When your child plays with friends he or she takes turns.
2. Your child can say, "My turn—your turn."
3. Your child works on taking turns with the toys.

Please acknowledge your child's efforts when he or she takes turns with others at home.

Thanks so much!

Sincerely,

_____

Sample Script: Sharing

The Issue

You may expect children to come to preschool knowing how to share, but many children do not know how to share. Children may need to be taught specifically how to share with their friends at school.

Overview

Many young children have never needed to share with siblings or peers. Sharing does not come naturally to human beings, so you must teach children how to share with peers.

Goals

◆ To teach children how to share so that they will have the opportunity to experience the rewards of friendships when they share with others

◆ To set the stage for successful classroom behavior and peer relationships when they enter elementary school

Solutions

The steps for teaching children to share are:

1. **Describe the social skill.**

   "Sometimes when you are playing with a toy, your friend wants to play with the same toy too. Children need to share with their friends."

   "When your friend wants the toy that you are playing with, you need to share with your friend. Say, 'Just a minute,' finish playing with the toy, and then give your friend the toy."

2. **Have the child describe social skill.**

   Ask the child, "What do you do when your friend wants the toy that you are playing with?"

   Child repeats what you explained earlier.

   Say, "Right, you say, 'Just a minute,' finish playing with the toy, and then give your friend the toy."

3. **Model the skill for the child.**

   Say, "Watch me. I am going to show you how to share." Model sharing a truck or doll with the child.

   Ask the child to say if you shared. Ask, "Did I share with you?"

   Child answers, "Yes."

   Say, "Right! I said, 'Just a minute,' I finished playing, and then I gave you the truck."

4. **The child models the skill with you.**

   Say, "Show me how you share."

   Say, "Good, you said, 'Just a minute.' You finished playing, and then you gave me the truck."

5. **Give an example of the social skill by modeling the skill with one of the child's peers.**

   Ask, "What did I do?"

   The child states what you did.

6. **The child demonstrates with peer.**

   Say, "Show me how share to with Joshua."

   (Child demonstrates with peer.)

   Say, "Great! You said, 'Just a minute.' You finished playing, and then you gave Joshua the truck."

Keys to Effective Classroom Management

♦ Unless you plan for transfer of learning, the child may not use the social skill that you are teaching her in the classroom. To do this you need to cue the child to share.

♦ Transfer of learning:

♦ Cue the child to use the social skill before it is needed. Before center play is a good time to remind the child to share.

♦ Involving parents in the use of the social skill will help the child to transfer learning to other people and situations. Send a note home to parents (see sample below) explaining the social skill that you are working on.

Sample Note to Parents

Dear Parents:

This week your child is working on the social skill of sharing. Please remind your child to share at home to support what we are teaching at school.

This is what your child is learning:

1. When a friend wants the toy that your child is using, he or she says, "Just a minute."
2. Your child finishes playing with the toy.
3. Then your child gives his or her friend the toy.

Please acknowledge your child's efforts when he or she shares with others at home.

Thanks so much!

Sincerely,

_____

The publisher grants permission for this page to be photocopied for classroom use only.

© Gryphon House, Inc. 800-638-0928. www.gryphonhouse.com

Sample Script: Sitting in Circle Time

The Issue

Structured learning times, when children must sit and respond at specific times, are difficult for some children. When children have difficulty sitting through Circle Time, for example, focus on teaching appropriate behavior during Circle Time rather than reprimanding the child.

Overview

When you model and teach appropriate behaviors for sitting in the learning circle, children learn what is expected. When children are punished for inappropriate behavior during Circle Time, they don't learn the appropriate behavior. Social skills, such as sitting during Circle Time, must be specifically taught to some children.

Goals

- ◆ To teach the child the appropriate behavior for sitting during Circle Time
- ◆ To teach the child to take part in a group setting

Solutions

The steps for teaching children to sit during Circle Time are:

1. **Describe the social skill.**

   Say, "When it is Circle Time, cross your legs on your mat, fold your hands, and say, 'criss—cross—applesauce.'"

2. **Have the child describe the social skill.**

   Ask the child, "What do you do when it is time to sit in circle?" Child states what she does when sitting in circle.

   Say, "Right, you cross your legs on your mat, fold your hands, and say, 'Criss—cross—applesauce.'"

3. **Model the behavior with the child.**

   Demonstrate and say, "Watch me. I am going to show you how to sit in Circle Time."

   Ask, "Did I sit in the circle in the right way?"

   The child answers, "Yes."

   Say, "Right, I crossed my legs on my mat, I folded my hands, and I said, 'Criss—cross—applesauce.'"

4. **The child models the behavior with you.**

   Say, "Show me how you sit in circle."

   Say, "Yes, you crossed your legs on your mat, you folded your hands, and you said, 'Criss—cross—applesauce.'"

5. **Model the behavior with another child.**

   Ask, "What did I do?"

   The child states what you did.

6. **The child demonstrates sitting in Circle Time.**

   Say, "Show me how to sit in Circle Time."

   (Child demonstrates on mat)

   Say, "Great! You crossed your legs on the mat, you folded your hands, and you said, 'Criss—cross—applesauce.'"

Keys to Effective Classroom Management

- ◆ Remember to cue the children about sitting in Circle Time, or any other time, appropriately. Say, "Remember criss—cross—applesauce. You cross your legs on your mat, you put your hands in your lap and you say, 'Criss—cross—applesauce.'" Acknowledge the children for sitting appropriately in the circle.
- ◆ Send a note home to parents (see sample on the next page) explaining the social skill that you are working on with the children.

Dear Parents:

This week your child is working on the social skill of sitting during Circle Time. Please ask your child to show you how he or she sits during Circle Time to support what we are teaching at school.

This is what your child is learning about sitting during Circle Time:

1. I cross my legs on my mat.
2. I fold my hands.
3. I say, "Criss—cross—applesauce."

Please acknowledge your child when he or she shows you how he or she sits during Circle Time.

Thanks so much!

Sincerely,

_____

Sample Script: Waiting in Line

The Issue

Waiting does not come naturally. By teaching children the appropriate way to wait in line, many problems can be prevented.

Overview

When children enter the preschool setting for the first time they must learn to wait in line. This is a skill that none of us enjoy—very few adults like to wait in line. However, it is a requirement for all of us, and it is particularly important when children enter school.

Goal

◆ To teach children what is expected of them when they wait in line. Later, when they enter elementary school, they will be able to wait without bothering others or disrupting the class. This is a good skill to teach to the entire class, or you can teach individual children who may have problems waiting in line.

Solutions

The steps for teaching children to wait in line are:

1. **Describe the social skill.**
   Say, "When we wait in line, we look at the person in front of us, we keep our hands to ourselves, and we stand tall."

2. **Have the child describe the social skill.**
   Ask the child, "What do I do when I wait in line?"
   Child states what you do when waiting in line.
   Say, "Right, I look straight ahead, I keep my hands to myself, and I stand tall."

3. **Model the behavior with the child.**
   Say, "Watch me. I am going to show you how to wait in line."
   Demonstrate in the place that you typically wait in line. When you say, "I keep my hands to myself," you can either fold your hands or put them to your side. Or say, "I put my bear in its cave" (putting hands behind you), or "I put my bee in its hive."

Exaggerate your posture when you say, "I stand tall."

Ask, "Did I wait in line properly?"

Child answers, "Yes."

Say, "Right! I looked straight ahead, I kept my hands to myself, and I stood tall."

4. **The child models with you.**

"Show me how you wait in line."

Say, "Good! You looked straight ahead, you kept your hands to yourself, and you stood tall."

5. **Give an example of social skill by modeling it appropriately with one of the child's peers and ask the child if you waited in line properly.**

Then ask, "What did I do?"

The child states what you did.

6. **The child demonstrates how to wait in line.**

Say, "Show me how to wait in line."

(Child demonstrates.)

"Great! You looked straight ahead, you kept your hands to yourself, and you stood tall."

Keys to Effective Classroom Management

◆ Make sure that you cue the children before it is time to stand in line and wait. It is important that you do not require children to wait for too long. How long children can wait depends on their age, their past experience, their temperament, and whether they have learned to wait quietly. The behaviors that you expect children to demonstrate will vary according to the situation. Some teachers expect children to wait in line quietly; others do not. A lot depends on their age and the situation. You can sing songs or do fingerplays while waiting, which makes the experience less difficult for children. The skill of waiting in line is different from walking in line with a group, which presents an additional need for instruction with young children.

◆ Transfer of learning:

◆ Cue the child to use the social skill before a situation occurs. Review the steps in waiting.

◆ Demonstrate with action figures, cars, dolls, and so on, how to wait in line.

◆ Send a note home to parents (see sample on the next page) explaining the social skill that you are working on:

Dear Parents:

This week your child is working on the social skill of how to wait in line. If you ask your child to show you how to wait in line, it will help us at school.

This is what your child is learning about waiting in line:

1. Look straight ahead.

2. Keep my hands to myself.

3. Stand tall.

Please acknowledge your child when he or she shows you how to wait in line. Your child can also show you how toys (animals, action figures, dolls, cars) wait in line.

Thanks so much!

Sincerely,

_____

Sample Script: Controlling Anger

The Issue

It is very important that children learn to control their tempers at a young age. As children get older, temper tantrums or inappropriate expressions of anger are tolerated less.

Overview

Controlling anger is an issue for many people. When children are young, tantrums and crying are typical. Some children may not have appropriate adult role models to show them how to get control of their anger. As mentioned earlier in this book, children need to learn to use words to express their feelings. But before they can do this they need to calm down so that they can learn how to express their feelings.

Goal

◆ To teach children how to calm down so that they can deal with their anger. Instead of acting on angry impulses, children will learn to use a self-control strategy.

Solutions

The steps to help children learn to control anger are:

1. **Describe the social skill.**

   Say, "When we get angry we may say or do things that can hurt other people. What we need to do instead is to cross our arms, take a deep breath, and say, 'control.'"

2. **Ask the child to describe the social skill.**

   Ask the child, "What do I need to do when I get angry?"

   Child crosses her arms, takes a deep breath, and says, "Control."

   Say, "Right, I cross my arms, take a deep breath, and say, 'Control.'"

3. **Model the behavior with the child.**

   Say, "Watch me: I am going to show you what to do when you get angry." (Demonstrate)

   Have child tell you what you did when you were angry.

   Ask, "Did I cross my arms, take a deep breath, and say, 'Control?'"

   Child answers, "Yes"

   Say, "Right! I crossed my arms, took a deep breath, and said, 'Control.'"

4. **The child models with you.**

   Say, "Show me what you need to do when you get angry."

   Child models with you.

   Say, "Yes, you crossed your arms, took a deep breath, and said, 'Control.'"

5. **Give a positive example of handling anger and ask the child if you did the right thing.**

   Ask, "What did I do?"

   The child states what you did.

6. **The child demonstrates what to do when angry.**

   Say, "Show me what you need to do when you get angry."

   (Child demonstrates.)

   "Yes. You crossed your arms, took a deep breath, and said, 'Control.'

Keys to Effective Classroom Management

◆ Children will need reminders to get control. Have children practice the skill before entering situations where they are likely to have problems with anger. Some children will need more practice and reminders than others.

◆ Cue the child to use the social skill when you see that she is becoming agitated. Don't wait for a meltdown to occur before reminding her to get "control."

◆ Send a note home to parents (see sample below) explaining the social skill that you are working on.

Sample Note to Parents

Dear Parents:

This week your child is working on the social skill of controlling anger. If you remind your child to do this when you see that he or she is becoming agitated, it will help us at school.

This is what your child is learning about what to do when he or she gets angry:
1. Cross my arms.
2. Take a deep breath.
3. Say, "Control."

Please acknowledge your child when he or she controls his or her anger (crosses his or her arms, takes a deep breath, and says, "Control").

Thanks so much!

Sincerely,

_____

A Lesson From a Turtle

The Issue

Young children are likely to react physically when they are angry or upset. They need to be taught ways to control physical urges to hit, kick, bite, or use words that hurt when they are agitated. By using this Turtle Technique (Joseph & Strain, 2003; Schneider, 1974), you show children how to control their body using the concrete example of "Mr. Turtle," who pulls his legs into his shell when he is upset. This is similar to the previous strategy for controlling anger.

Overview

Children need a meaningful example of how to control physical urges to hit, bite, or kick when upset. By using the turtle example, you are able to combine science instruction with social skills instruction. This provides a concrete and memorable way of instructing young children in controlling their tendencies toward aggression.

Goal

◆ To teach children to use self-control instead of aggression when they are upset. The Turtle Technique is one way that children can gain self-control. The goal is for children to become self-managed and socially adept.

Solutions

The Turtle Technique:

1. As a class activity, observe a real turtle or a videotape of a turtle.
2. Ask the children to watch and see what the turtle does when he is upset.
3. Ask, "What does Mr. Turtle do when he is upset?"
4. Encourage children to notice that the turtle tucks his legs in when he is upset.
5. As a class, pretend to be turtles: bring in arms and legs, and tuck in heads.
6. Ask the children how Mr. Turtle feels when he is inside his shell. (quiet, peaceful)
7. Ask the children to practice "playing turtle" when you ring a bell.
8. Ask the children what happens when they are upset or angry. What might they do with their arms? (hit) What could they do with their legs? (kick) What might they do with their mouths? (use mean words or bite)
9. Show the children how they can do what Mr. Turtle does when he is upset—tuck in their arms, tuck in their legs, close their mouths, and calm down.
10. Play the turtle game whenever you ring a bell during the school day.
11. During the school day, cue children to calm down "like Mr. Turtle" when you see them becoming agitated.

Keys to Effective Classroom Management

◆ This process takes time and instruction. Do not let children play with real turtles due to the risk of salmonella. However, when you show the children a box turtle and house it in a secure container for observation in the classroom, children are interested and ready learners of this technique. Note that box turtles should not be kept in captivity for extended periods of time. The concrete example of the turtle makes the lesson in self-control age-appropriate and understandable for young children.

Use of Distractions

The Issue

Waiting or remaining seated for even five minutes may be a long time for a young child. Providing a distraction enables children to stay engaged for a longer period of time.

Overview

Even adults sometimes have difficulty remaining calm while waiting in line at the bank, waiting at the doctor's office, and sitting in the dentist's chair. It is not surprising that children have difficulty with some situations, such as waiting or sitting still for a period of time. Like adults, young children also need to have something to do while they wait or remain seated for what seems like a long time to them.

Goal

◆ To enable children to stay engaged for progressively longer periods of time. With the use of a distraction, children will not need to use negative behavior to escape an activity that they do not like.

Solutions

This technique is best used with negative behaviors that have the pay-off of escaping an activity that children are tired of or do not like. Some of the most common situations are waiting or remaining seated for Circle Time or a large-group activity. The steps to help children learn to stay engaged are:

1. Determine that the child's negative behavior has the purpose of avoiding a situation or task.

2. Observe the child and the classroom to see if there are toys or objects that she enjoys that she could hold. Toys that have soothing sensory characteristics are good. Examples of good "feely toys" that the child can hold on to during periods of time where she needs to wait or remain seated include small stuffed animals or beanie babies, textured rubber toys such as a hedgehog, and stuffed/weighted snakes. Books also are good to use while children wait.

3. When it is time for the child to wait or remain seated, give the child the toy, book, or other preferred item to hold.

4. Acknowledge the child for waiting and sitting quietly.

Keys to Effective Classroom Management

◆ Distractions are effective for young children and for older children with limited attention spans.

Using "Time Out" Appropriately

The Issue

Currently, many teachers use "time out" as a technique for teaching children to manage themselves. Unfortunately, time out is often misused, and children have little understanding about why they are sent to the time-out chair.

Overview

Any classroom management strategy needs to be carefully planned and explained to children to prevent confusion about its use.

Goal

◆ To use appropriate time-out procedures that will help children understand that they are in control of their own behaviors and that will help children to become independent learners and thinkers

Solutions

The time-out chair is a place in the classroom designed to help children regain their composure and emotions. If you use time out as a punishment, then the chair is being misused. Here are some tips for improving the use of time out:

◆ Designate a specific chair to be used for time out.

◆ Explain to children what time out means and demonstrate the chair's use to children.

◆ When you send a child to time-out, explain why she is being sent to the time-out chair.

◆ Keep the child in the time-out chair for a short period to time (the age of the child is a good rule of thumb—three minutes for a three-year-old; four minutes for a four-year-old; and so on).

◆ Ask the child if she has regained her composure or controlled her emotions. If she says, "yes," allow her to return to her normal activities. If she says, "no," talk to her about how to control herself when she is with groups of other children.

◆ When the child is ready to return to normal classroom activity, give her a chance to return to her original play experience.

◆ If the child behaves inappropriately again, talk more seriously to the child and ask her to choose another activity to participate in.

Keys to Effective Classroom Management

◆ Whenever "time out" is used, children need explanations to assist in their understanding of autonomy and self-regulation.

◆ Time out should not be used if the child is attempting to avoid an activity or to provide a break from a difficult child.

◆ Children should never be restrained (strapped in) a time-out chair. Not only is this demeaning and non-instructive, but it violates most state laws regarding the use of restraints.

Listening With the Entire Body

The Issue

Many children have difficulty sitting at Circle Time or other times when it is important for them to sit quietly, attend to the speaker, and listen. Children may not understand intuitively how to listen. If children learn the behaviors necessary for good listening, they are more likely to understand the task and act appropriately.

Overview

Listening involves not just our ears, but our entire bodies. You can provide instruction to children to show them what they need to do in order to be effective listeners. By teaching listening skills, you are able to focus on the appropriate behaviors that children need to learn, rather than focusing on negative behavior and administering consequences. As always, it is better to be proactive than reactive.

Goal

◆ To teach children specifically what they need to do to listen (such as at Circle Time and all other times when children must listen to instruction without disruptions) so they will learn how to be effective listeners

Solutions

Explain to the children that they are going to learn to be good listeners. Use the script outlined below.

1. Good listeners know how to listen with their whole bodies. They listen with seven body parts. Can you guess what body parts are used to listen? (Solicit additional answers from the children.)
   Ears: We open our ears when we listen.
   Eyes: We look at the person speaking when we listen.
   Mouth: Our mouths are closed when we listen.
   Hands: Our hands are folded in our laps when we listen.
   Feet: Our feet are on the floor when we listen.
   Seat: Our seats are in the chair (or on our mat, carpet square, etc.) when we listen.
   Brain: We turn our brains on (click) and think about what the speaker is saying when we listen.

2. Model listening, describing what you are doing with each of your seven body parts

3. Say to the children, "Show me how we listen. We open our ears (click and gesture). We look at the speaker (gesture). We close our mouth (exaggerated demonstration). We put our hands in our lap (gesture). We put our feet on the floor (gesture). We put our seats in the chair (gesture). We turn on our brains and listen (click and gesture)." Children demonstrate listening behaviors.

4. "Wow! What great listeners I see. Let's listen closely to _____(brief story, poem, song, etc.)"

Keys to Effective Classroom Management

◆ After teaching listening behaviors, keep the listening activity that follows brief and engaging, ensuring the children's success. Then acknowledge the children for being good listeners. After they have demonstrated good listening (by staying quiet and sitting during instruction) you can ask questions and acknowledge children for being good listeners when they are able to answer questions about the story, song, game, and so on. Long Circle Times are not developmentally appropriate for young children. Be aware of how long children are expected to sit.

181

Collaborative Activity

The Issue

Most adults know that it helps to have company when they have to do something unpleasant, difficult, or boring. It is never as hard to complete an unwanted task if you have help. Young children feel the same way. When you ask them to pick up toys or clean up a mess (even if it looks like a small job), it may seem like a big job to the child. When you help the child with the task, then she is able to get the job done. At other times, children may be reluctant to complete a task or project. If you assist the child in completing it, then the child learns to make a good effort and take pride in her accomplishments.

Overview

Although you may like to think that your classroom is so engaging that children will not find tasks unpleasant, this will not always be the case. Children need to take responsibility in an age-appropriate way for the small tasks in the classroom, even those that they may find distasteful. They need to learn to pick up after themselves and clean up their own messes. If you can help the child to start a new activity, she may actually find it enjoyable.

Goals

- To help children to improve their ability to complete tasks that they find unpleasant, boring, or threatening because they are new
- To reduce power struggles in the classroom

Solutions

Consider the following when encouraging children to do tasks that they might find unpleasant:

- This technique is most useful when children refuse to complete tasks.
- It is particularly appropriate with negative behavior that children use to escape tasks that they find unpleasant.
- Monitor your own attitude and stay positive and enthusiastic.
- Examples:
  - For picking up blocks, say, "You pick up the big blocks and I will pick up the little ones."
  - For picking up crayons, "You pick up the long ones and I will pick up the broken ones."
  - For a new type of art project, "You paint and I will fold the paper."
- Many times, the child just needs a little help getting started.
- As the child gets better at completing tasks, have her assume more of the work as you do less.

Keys to Effective Classroom Management

- It is critical to avoid power struggles with children. When you are able to stay positive and enthusiastic, children will be more motivated to complete the task. This technique is not intended as manipulation, but rather a way to teach positive social behavior to children who might otherwise demonstrate serious classroom behavior problems.

Warm-Up Activity

The Issue

Some children are resistant to following directions for different reasons: there are other activities that the child prefers, the activity is new, or they do not understand what they need to do. When you use a warm-up activity before making a request for something that children find difficult or unpleasant, children are more likely to respond positively.

Overview

This strategy is based on the behavioral principle that human beings respond to: people need to adjust to a situation before demands are made. Sometimes young children are expected to comply with directives with little time to adjust to the situation or person. Salespeople know the principle of using warm-up activities. They do not ask customers to buy something before engaging in conversation. Then they ask questions that are likely to get positive answers.

Goal

◆ To use a warm-up activity so that children will learn to respond positively to directions that they might not find appealing

Solutions

This method works well with children who are sometimes described as oppositional or noncompliant. When a child demonstrates negative behavior to escape a task, a warm-up activity may be appropriate.

1. Get to know the child well enough to determine how to proceed. For example, you know that the child is likely to refuse to put the dinosaurs away. You also know that she enjoys playing with them and can follow directions during play, such as, "Make the dinosaur walk," "Make the dinosaur jump," and "Make the dinosaur eat."

2. Give three quick requests that the child can easily follow such as, "Make the dinosaur walk," "Make the dinosaur jump," and "Make the dinosaur eat."

3. After the child has enjoyed playing and following your directions, ask the child to perform the task you wish, for example, "Make the dinosaur disappear into the cave." Then show the child how to put all the dinosaurs back in the "cave."

4. Other examples include:

   ◆ Have a brief exercise period in a circle outside. Have the children follow simple group instructions, such as jump, march, stretch—then ask them to line up to come in from the playground.

   ◆ Ask the children to identify simple body parts on themselves—then request that they sit on their mats for group time.

   ◆ Ask the child to give you "five" with her right hand, give you "five" with her left hand, and give you a hug—then lie down on her cot for a nap.

5. Be sure to affirm the child for following directions.

Keys to Effective Classroom Management

◆ The purpose of this method is to teach social behaviors that will benefit children. This method enables you to avoid a power struggle and to establish appropriate social behaviors.

Grandma's Rule

The Issue

Grandma's Rule goes like this: Finish your green beans, and then you may have dessert. Grandma's Rule is also known as the Premack Principle: a non-preferred activity is more likely to be completed if it is followed by a preferred activity (Maag, 2004; Premack, 1959). When you schedule activities while considering this principle, you are likely to have a classroom that runs more smoothly.

Overview

All people have their likes and dislikes. No one can go through life only doing enjoyable things. When your classroom schedule alternates low-preference and high-preference activities, children are more likely to demonstrate socially appropriate behavior.

Goal

◆ To develop a classroom schedule that minimizes negative behavior through the use of Grandma's Rule: low-preference activities are followed by high-preference activities

Solutions

Consider the following steps:

1. Determine the times of the day when behavior problems are most likely to occur. Some examples might include low-preference activities such as clean-up time, times when children need to remain seated, and transition times.
2. Determine the daily activities that children anticipate. These might include outdoor free play, centers, snacks, music, and mealtimes.
3. Develop a schedule in which low-preference activities are followed by high-preference activities.
4. When it is time to clean up or sit down for an activity, remind the children that they will go to the playground, lunch, or the desired activity after they complete the task at hand.
5. Acknowledge the children for their good behavior during the more difficult task.

Keys to Effective Classroom Management

◆ Although circle time is interesting and engaging, sitting is a task that many young children find difficult. When your schedule alternates quiet or sedentary activities with active play, you will better meet the needs of children who find it hard to sit. Children with ADHD need to have only a short period of in-seat activities followed by active learning. When they are better able to handle sitting, then the period of time can be lengthened. Beware of expecting too much too soon. Remember, too, that children are individuals with different preferences and dislikes.

Delay Cues

The Issue

When you use delay cues, you enable children to gain more self-control so that they can stay engaged for a longer period of time.

Overview

Most people attend meetings or other gatherings where delay cues such as "Just a minute and we will be finished" or "I just have one more point to talk about and then you can go home" are used. These cues enable people to stay engaged when they know that the meeting is going to end soon. A good speaker uses delay cues to keep the audience from becoming restless. You can use delay cues effectively in the classroom.

Goal

◆ To enable children to increase their attention span and stay on task longer by using delay cues

Solutions

Use this technique when a child exhibits negative behavior to escape a task that she finds difficult or unpleasant.

1. Observe the child to determine which tasks during the day are difficult for her (those where she is likely to behave negatively).

2. See how long the child will persist with the task before becoming agitated.

3. Once you know how long a child can tolerate a task or activity, then give the child a delay cue at the point where she just begins to get restless.

4. A delay cue goes like this, "Just one minute and then you can get up," "We're almost finished—just one minute and then you can have a snack," and "Two more minutes and then we're done."

5. Once the child is used to the delay cues, start increasing the time or amount of the task before moving on. Examples include: "Just two minutes and then we're finished," "We're almost finished—just five minutes until snack," and "Only three more and then we're done."

Keys to Effective Classroom Management

◆ Easy does it! When you use a delay cue, you may be pushing the child beyond her current limit. Do not expect too much too soon. Timing is very important—watch carefully for the point where the child is just beginning to become restless or agitated. It is important to make the expectation manageable. When children are asked to do too much too soon, a "meltdown" may result—something that everyone wants to avoid. If the child is unusually agitated, if the child is not feeling well, or if there were difficulties earlier in the day, be especially careful in expecting the child to continue in the activity.

Helping Friends

The Issue

To improve a child's behavior, pair her with a socially skilled peer who will be a role model and elicit appropriate social behavior. Often children learn best from peers with similar characteristics who are well liked in the classroom.

Overview

The power of observational learning has been recognized for many years. Social Learning Theory is built on the fact that human beings learn through observation and imitation (Maag, 2004). Young children are astute observers and imitators—and often they observe and imitate behaviors that you would prefer them not to! However, this ability of young children to observe and imitate their peers can be a powerful force in the classroom when children with problem behavior are paired with peers who have strong social skills.

Goal

◆ To enable children to learn appropriate social behavior through peer partners in the classroom

Solutions

Consider the following steps:

1. Select several socially competent peers for peer partners. Important characteristics to look for in the peer partner include a positive attitude, the ability to get along with others, good language skills, and motivation to be helpful. Good general health and attendance helps, as well.

2. Pair the child with the peer partner during times when there is opportunity for social interaction such as center time or outdoor play.

3. During structured group activities such as Circle Time, place the child with problem behavior between two socially skilled peers.

4. Make sure that you have several children to serve as peer partners—otherwise the peer partner ends up with too much responsibility and may resent the child with behavioral difficulties.

5. Explain to the peer partner that she can help her friend learn to play. Explain that she can help by showing her friend the specific skill. Model the skill so that she knows what to do.

6. Tell the peer partner to be sure to ask you if she needs help.

7. Affirm the peer partner for being a good helper. Thank her for helping her friend.

Keys to Effective Classroom Management

◆ Children often learn skills more easily from peers than they do from direct instruction from adults. When you enlist peer partners, rotate them so that no one becomes tired of the responsibility. Dealing with a child with problem behavior can be just as difficult for children as for you. Acknowledge the children for working well together, and let them know how much you appreciate them.

Enlisting Parents

The Issue

Parents know their children better than anyone else. When you enlist the help of parents, you are working with the only people who will be there continuously throughout the child's life. When parents and teachers work together to teach the child appropriate social behavior, the child benefits.

Overview

When parents help to support a behavior change plan, the child is more likely to be able to transfer the desired social behavior to other people and places.

Goals

- To develop a parent-teacher partnership to help children improve their behavior
- To promote a lasting change in behavior that transfers to other settings besides the school

Solutions

Consider the following:

- Make sure that the parents understand from the beginning that you want to teach their child how to get along in the classroom, not reprimand her for what she does not know how to do.
- Before developing the behavior improvement plan, talk with the parents to gain their perspective on the situation.
- Find out from parents the child's likes and dislikes. This helps in understanding her current behavior and knowing how to reward appropriate behavior.
- Determine how the parents prefer to be contacted, and the best way to communicate what you are working on at school.
- Send home notes or videotapes on a regular basis to describe the social skills that the child is working on.
- When asking the parents to work on a social skill, be specific in describing the skill and what you expect them to do.
- Always remember to thank the parents for their help.

Keys to Effective Classroom Management

- Enlist parents as partners rather than blame them for their child's lack of social skills. Remember that parents have outside pressure of other children, jobs, marital difficulties, and financial worries. These pressures may reduce the parent's ability to support the child in improving her behavior. Never give up on a child because the parents have problems—many children have learned to behave appropriately at school even with a chaotic home life. However, when parents and the school work together, it increases the chances of the child learning to transfer the social skills that she learns at school into the home setting.

Social Stories and Literature

The Issue

Stories that highlight social skills have been used to teach social skills to children with autism and developmental disabilities. In this technique, you develop a story to describe the social situation, explain the appropriate social behavior, present the viewpoint of others, and help the child remember what to do in the situation.

Overview

Some children have not learned the social behavior appropriate to situations. The use of a story explains the situation explicitly and lays out the expected behavior. For those children who are unable to tune in to the important aspects of social behaviors, this type of instruction is useful.

Goals

◆ To help children understand the social situation, to see others' viewpoints, and to use appropriate social behavior in the situation when needed

Solutions

To develop a story that highlights or illustrates a specific social skill, use the following steps:

1. Using two to five sentences, describe what people do in a social situation. These are known as *descriptive* sentences.

2. Describe the child's appropriate response in positive, observable terms. This is the *directive* sentence.

3. The next type of sentence is the *perspective* sentence. It describes others' reactions to the situation so that the child can understand their viewpoints.

4. After you have read the story with or to the child, develop the final sentence with the child. This is the *control* sentence. It helps the child to remember what to do in the social situation.

5. Examples include:

   ◆ The children are playing in centers. They are having fun with the toys. The teacher starts singing the "clean-up" song. The children start to pick up their toys and put them on the shelves.

   ◆ I am playing with the cars in the transportation center. I like to play with cars. The teacher starts singing the "clean-up" song. I stop playing and put the cars on the shelf.

   ◆ The teacher smiles when she sees everyone cleaning up. She says that we will get to go outside when we finish cleaning up. The teacher likes it when the children pick up their toys.

   ◆ I know that when I hear the "clean-up" song that it is time to pick up toys.

6. You can use pictures or photographs to illustrate the story.

7. Read the story each day with the child, pointing to the words as you read them.

Keys to Effective Classroom Management

◆ Stories can be used to teach children social skills, how to complete an activity, or what will happen during the day. They are particularly helpful with children who have not learned through observing the environment. Social stories can be written for a variety of skills and situations. They can be used individually or with a group. When using a social story with the group, you can present it on chart paper, on a single page, or in a folder.

Putting It Into Practice: Billy

The principles supporting this narrative are:

- Classroom management requires teachers to deal with individual problems.
- When one technique fails, try another.
- Some children respond quickly, while others require a longer time to respond.
- Involve the family as much as possible when dealing with a child's problems.
- Sharing personal experiences will facilitate children's understanding of their own problems.
- Children may need instruction about expressing their feelings before they can verbalize their needs and concerns.
- Professional assistance beyond the classroom is necessary on occasion.
- Patience and good humor are essential to success.

Miss Carolyn looked across the playground as Mason, sobbing, approached her. "Billy pushed me out of the sandbox, and he says I can't play," he cried. Miss Carolyn took a few minutes to comfort Mason and then went to the sandbox to see what was happening. There was Billy, playing calmly with all of the sand toys.

Miss Carolyn explained to Billy that he needed to share the toys with Mason. "But I want to play with them. I don't want to share," Billy replied.

Miss Carolyn explained to Billy that he needed to share and that Mason wanted to play, too. She reintroduced Mason to the sandbox and encouraged the boys to take turns. She talked about how Billy hurt Mason's feelings when he pushed him out of the sandbox and explained how someone could get hurt. When the boys were busy playing she diverted her attention to the slide to make sure that the children were following the safety rules. Within a few minutes Mason was back again, crying because Billy hit him and told him to get out.

This scene was played out in similar ways in several different activities with Billy. It was more than simply not sharing toys. Billy physically hurt other children, and then they gave him whatever he wanted. He could simply give them a "mean look" and they put the toy down. Sometimes he would puff up and saunter over to one of his classmates, and the other child left the center as he approached. Billy was able to play with any toy that he wanted without the interference of other children. Miss Carolyn remembered the first week of kindergarten. Other children had tattled on Billy, and she had discouraged the tattling. She realized that she should have confronted his behavior earlier in the school year, but she knew that there was still time to help Billy learn to interact appropriately at school. After all, this was kindergarten!

Miss Carolyn spent the next week watching Billy from a short distance on the playground and in centers. She observed that, generally, he would share when she was within a few feet of him. But when she turned her back or began helping others, there were problems. Billy grabbed toys, pushed others out of the way to get on the swings, and hit classmates with blocks as he entered the Block Center. Miss Carolyn typically had to comfort the

(continued on the next page)

victim, enabling Billy to play with the toys of his choice. Because of the "fear factor," the other children gave him whatever he wanted with only a look or threatening body language. She observed that he told the other children to "leave my trucks alone" even when he was not in the Transportation Center, and they avoided the trucks. The pay-off for Billy's behavior was the freedom to use the toys without interference from others.

Miss Carolyn first decided to teach Billy the appropriate way to ask to play with the toys. She demonstrated the appropriate sequence for him, and he showed her how to ask for toys with her and with a classmate. Before entering centers or the playground, she cued him about how to ask for toys. She discussed the classroom rules: take turns, be kind to others, and finish your work. She also reminded him that "people are not for hitting," and that "people are not for pushing." When the children went to centers or the playground, she visually monitored Billy. She encouraged peers with strong social skills to play in his area. Whenever his body language indicated that he might be getting ready to become aggressive, she approached his area and reminded him of the rules.

The other children also needed some instruction in dealing with Billy. Miss Carolyn used a whole group lesson to show the children what to do when someone tried to take your toy. They were instructed to say, "Wait. I am playing with the _____ now. You play with this one (point to alternative toy)." When on the playground or in centers, she encouraged them to tell their friends to wait if they had not finished playing with the toy. She also worked with the class on learning to wait.

Miss Carolyn thought about some of her classroom practices that might promote aggressive behavior. She realized that Billy rarely had his picture on the "good work wall" and that he was large for his age and poorly coordinated. She decided that the atmosphere of individual competition, with the emphasis on prizes for the best behavior, the best writing, or the best picture excluded Billy and several other children as well. Miss Carolyn decided to have children work more often with a buddy and to display everyone's work.

Also, she realized that her practice of using the "thinking chair" was inappropriate and ineffective. When Billy was there, he usually sang, giggled, and gestured to make the other children laugh. She realized that he lacked the ability to get positive attention from others. The "thinking chair" really served as a reward for Billy rather than a disciplinary measure since he was the star of the show in the thinking chair. Miss Carolyn took the

"thinking chair" out of the classroom, and decided to give Billy some classroom responsibilities that would enable him to be helpful and interact with others. She learned that he could successfully pass out papers, snacks, and sharpen broken crayons. Rather than using the thinking chair, she made Billy come in early from the playground with the assistant. If he grabbed toys during centers, she made that center off limits for him for the rest of center time. Occasionally, she had to close centers for a few days until the children were able to play appropriately with the toys.

In addition to these actions, Miss Carolyn set up a parent conference with Ms. Thomas, Billy's mother. She learned that Billy was the middle child and that he tried to compete with his older brother. The mother expressed concern that Billy's father took pride in the fact that Billy was "tough" and could "stick up for himself," even with his older brother. With the new baby at home this year Billy also feeling somewhat displaced. Ms. Thomas realized that Billy was not as "tough" as his father believed or as independent as she had assumed. Billy's mother decided to spend some special time with him each night before bed. She also realized that she would need to monitor both of her sons' play more closely. Perhaps Billy was not able to compete as successfully with his older brother as she had believed.

There was not a single simple solution for Billy. His behavior did not change quickly. Much of Miss Carolyn's effort went into preventing Billy from "bullying" his classmates. Miss Carolyn's plan for Billy involved many factors: teaching Billy appropriate behaviors, teaching classmates how to respond, increased supervision and monitoring, decreasing competition in the classroom so that everyone was a "winner," working with peer buddies, providing Billy with classroom responsibilities, changing her discipline measures for Billy, and meeting with his parents. Even with these measures, Miss Carolyn still had to monitor and adjust her plan as Billy and his classmates responded. However, she realized that by the end of kindergarten, Billy had made several friends and his aggressive behaviors typically occurred only on a weekly basis rather than numerous times per day. At the end of the school year Miss Carolyn was saddened at the thought of Billy going off to first grade. After all, she had invested so much in this child and she had seen how much he had grown and changed. Even with all of the hard work, she thought to herself, "If I have another child like Billy in my class next year it will be fine with me. He is one of my shining stars."

Communication Skills

**Chapter
9**

Many children who exhibit troubling behavior have problems with communication. This may occur across several dimensions. Children may have difficulty expressing themselves or understanding the communication of others. Children also may have problems with either verbal or nonverbal communication. This chapter addresses all four of these areas and focuses on interpreting and expressing feelings. Young children have strong feelings, but, often, they do not know how to express themselves. Children may not be able to comprehend how others are feeling. This is a developmental phenomenon. As they grow, however, sensitive adults can help children understand how others feel.

Some common communication skills are addressed in this chapter. Among these skills are:

- asking for help
- gaining attention
- asking for permission
- asking for a toy
- asking a friend to play
- asking for an activity

When children have these communication skills, they are less likely to use challenging behavior to get what they need.

Finally, the use of nonverbal communication is also addressed. Some authorities believe that most of the content of our communication messages is nonverbal. Rarely do children receive direct instruction about their nonverbal communication, yet teachers expect them to have learned it. The goal of this chapter is to teach children to be effective communicators, both verbally and nonverbally. This is a critical component of language development.

Communication and Behavior: The Dynamic Duo

The Issue

When you teach children appropriate ways to communicate and assist them in using their communication skills, you are helping them get better control of their behavior.

Overview

Many young children with behavior problems have difficulty with communication. For some of these children the difficulty with communication is a skill problem: They lack the verbal skills to communicate their wants and needs in socially acceptable ways. For others, the difficulty is a performance problem: they are able to communicate verbally, but for some reason they do not do it.

Goal

◆ To teach children to use their words to express themselves, rather than communicate their needs in negative ways

Solutions

The steps to improving children's communication skills are:

1. Analyze the behavior problem to determine the pay-off (see page 136).
2. Determine a "fair-pair" behavior (see page 159) that is a verbal skill: what could the child say to get his needs met instead of the negative behavior?
3. Observe the child to see if he uses this verbal skill some of the time. If the child has the capability of using the verbal skill, then you know that it is a performance problem, not a skill problem. In this case, you want to cue the child to use the skill at a time when he is likely to have problem behaviors.
4. If the child does not currently demonstrate the verbal skill, then design a teaching plan so that he can learn the acceptable verbal behavior. The next sections of this chapter are dedicated to teaching appropriate verbal behaviors to children.
5. After the child has learned the verbal skill, prompt him to use it.
6. Praise him for using his words.

Keys to Effective Classroom Management

◆ You might overhear teachers say, "He knows what to do, but he chooses not to do it." Be cautious about concluding that a child "chooses" not to do the right thing. For most children who know what to do yet don't do it, this is not simply a decision. The child more likely has the behavior in some situations, but has not transferred it to other situations. More often than not, the behavior has worked for him in some situations and not in others. You must show the child that the acceptable social behavior works for him at school—and you must be sure that the negative behavior does not work at all when he is at school.

General Principles in Teaching Social Communication

The Issue

Show children how to use appropriate social communication. When you teach verbal skills, first use imitation, and then cue the child less over time as he becomes better able to communicate verbally.

Overview

When teaching young children social behavior, one of the most successful teaching techniques involves verbal imitation with cues to the child. This teaching method makes that child more independent in his communication and less reliant on you for instruction.

Goal

◆ To help children learn to communicate their needs spontaneously in a socially acceptable manner

Solutions

Consider the following steps:

1. When teaching a social-verbal skill to a young child, make sure that it is short and simple. For example, if you want the child to learn to ask (rather than grab), say, "May I have a cookie, please?" If the child does not have the ability to use a sentence that long, you can shorten it to "Cookie, please?"

2. When you first begin to teach the social-verbal skill, model the skill using exaggerated facial expressions, intonation, and gestures.

3. Ask the child to say, "May I have a cookie, please?" while you hold the cookies.

4. After the child is able to do this, hold up the cookies and wait for the child to ask. Wait and look at him with expectation.

5. If the child does not ask for the cookie, say, "Tell me what you want." Wait and look at him with expectation.

6. If the child still does not respond, to the child say, "Say, 'Cookie, please.'" Then give him the cookie when he asks.

7. Recognize and be aware of the child's level of language development. For children with very delayed language, affirm their attempts to communicate verbally, although their articulations and pronunciation are immature. For children with minimal verbal skills, refer to the section "Sign Language and Gestures" on page 212.

Keys to Effective Classroom Management

◆ Never get into a power struggle with a child about communication! There are few things that you can make a child do, and one of them is speak. The best way to avoid a power struggle is to watch your attitude and tone of voice. If you sound like a drill sergeant and use your "teacher voice" the child may become oppositional. Instead, keep your manner positive and upbeat—monitor your attitude!

Labeling Emotions

The Issue

Before children can express their feelings, they need to learn how to identify their emotions.

Overview

Young children sometimes are not able to express their emotions in positive ways. Children (and also some adults) have not learned to identify their feelings and have no way of expressing how they feel in words. Receptive labeling of expressions is an essential ability that some children must be taught explicitly if they are to learn to express their feelings.

Goal

◆ To help children learn to identify feelings in themselves and others

Solutions

Consider the following steps when teaching children to identify their emotions:

1. Look through your picture file, books, and magazines. Find several realistic pictures that identify each of the basic feelings: happy, sad, angry, surprised, and scared.

2. Starting with two "feeling pictures," have the children label the pictures as happy or sad.

3. Sort the pictures into the happy pile and the sad pile, labeling each picture as you place it. Then have the child sort the pictures into the happy pile and the sad pile, while you label them. As the child starts to label them verbally, speak more softly.

4. Practice this until the child can sort and label the pictures.

5. Add a set of pictures to identify another emotion.

6. Identify the emotion. Using one of the previous sets of "feeling pictures," sort the two sets of pictures as you did earlier.

7. When the child is able to sort and label the two sets of feeling pictures, you can sort the three sets that you have learned.

8. Repeat this process with the other sets of feeling pictures until the child is able to identify all five feelings.

9. It is best to work one-on-one with a child and for short periods of time. If you work on it for just a few minutes each day you will likely be more successful.

Keys to Effective Classroom Management

◆ When teaching children to identify feelings, start small. Begin with simple pictures of only two feelings—usually the easiest ones are happy, sad, and angry. Short periods of time work best. Although this is an excellent group activity, the child with problem behavior will benefit from individual instruction for short periods before doing the activity with the group.

Expressing Emotions

The Issue

If you teach children to recognize emotions, then it is easier for them to learn to express feelings during a strong emotional state. During periods of strong emotions, it is difficult to maintain attention and learn new concepts.

Overview

Children experience strong emotions, but they are often unable to express themselves if they do not know what they are feeling. Once children learn to identify emotions, then they are better able to express their feelings when they are experiencing strong emotions.

Goal

- To teach children how to identify when they are happy, sad, angry, surprised, or scared, so they will be able to say how they feel

Solutions

Consider the following:

- Work on identifying emotions by making faces in the mirror.
- Identify feelings as the children demonstrate them during the day.
- Start talking about why people feel sad, angry, and so on, as you describe the feelings of the children during the day.
- After the child is able to identify emotions in pictures and in the mirror, then he is likely to be better able to express his feelings as they actually occur.
- Practice demonstrating emotions and labeling them using a mirror.
- When the child demonstrates happiness, sadness, anger, etc., during the day, describe how he feels. For example, "Mason, you look sad—what happened?"
- As the child demonstrates feelings (and before he becomes really agitated), ask the child about his strong feelings. Encourage the child to tell how he feels.
- If the child is not able to describe how he feels, then you can ask if he feels sad, happy, and so on.
- Make a "Feeling Book" for each child and discuss a different feeling each day. Children can find pictures of things that make them happy, sad, or other emotions. They can tell you what makes them angry, happy, and so on, and you can write it in their Feeling Book.
- Asking parents to help children find pictures for their Feeling Book is an excellent way to involve parents in the process.

Keys to Effective Classroom Management

- Always honor the child's feelings. However, this does not excuse inappropriate behavior. Talk about the child's feelings and acknowledge why he feels as he does, but explain what he needs to do. For example, "I know you are angry when it is time to pick up blocks. You were having fun playing and you don't want to pick up. But we need to pick up even when we don't like it. That way our toys will be easier to use later. We can go outside after we pick up."

Gaining Attention

The Issue

You are in the unique position of changing and preventing children's challenging behaviors. Many times children who learn appropriate behaviors at school are able to transfer them to their homes and communities. There are specific strategies that are effective when dealing with challenging behaviors that are attention-seeking in nature.

Overview

Many young children use negative behaviors to get their parents' or teacher's attention. All too often, these children find that their negative behaviors are very effective in gaining the adult's attention. Even when the attention that children receive consists of scolding or reprimands, they are getting attention. For some children this is the only attention that they receive from adults. Indeed, negative adult attention may look like "love" to this child. When you reward children with attention for negative behavior, it not only continues, but often becomes worse.

Goal

- To teach children appropriate ways of gaining attention. As children learn appropriate attention-seeking behaviors, they may find that the negative behaviors are no longer useful.

Solutions

Teaching children appropriate ways to gain adult attention is most effective when used in conjunction with other preventive strategies.

- One preventive strategy is to give the child plenty of high-quality attention early in the day when he is behaving appropriately. Give lots of attention throughout the day as long as he demonstrates appropriate behavior.
- Vary the type of attention. Some children prefer pats on the back, play interaction, smiles, or verbal comments. Observe the child's reaction to the type of attention that you provide.
- Make sure that negative behaviors are invalid and ineffective in getting attention. Do not scold the child, do not interact verbally, and do not provide eye contact when the child uses negative behavior to get your attention.
- Provide activities in which the child will be successful. Look at what the child likes to do in his free time. Look for the child's gifts and talents. Showcase these abilities. Give the child plenty of attention when engaged in these activities.
- Teach the child positive ways to recruit your attention, including using the following phrases: "Look at this," "Come here, please," "Watch me," and "Miss ___" (addressing the adult by name).
- Use the following steps:
  1. Explain to the child that when he wants your attention, he needs to let you know by saying, "Miss ___" (or "Look at this," and so on). Select one phrase at a time for instruction.
  2. Model the skill, using a gesture along with the verbal request.
  3. Prompt the child to imitate the skill.
  4. Give the child attention and praise for requesting attention.
  5. Rehearse the appropriate way to get attention.
  6. Prompt the child to recruit attention.
  7. Combine the verbal request with a gesture—then you can use the gesture as a prompt for the verbal request.

Keys to Effective Classroom Management

- The goal is to teach children how to get attention appropriately while making their negative attention-seeking behavior ineffective and invalid. Success takes time and effort, but it pays off. Persistence is vital to success.

198

Asking for Help

The Issue

When you see that children are becoming frustrated, prompt children to ask for help. This is preferable to a tantrum or children giving up.

Overview

Children become frustrated when they are not able to accomplish what they want to do. As young children they often lack the skills that they need to complete tasks and they become frustrated. This is a common cause of classroom behavior problems.

Goal

♦ To teach children to ask for help, enabling them to complete tasks and avoid negative behavior

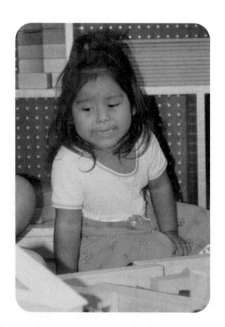

Solutions

Consider the following suggested script:

1. **Describe the social skill.**

   Say, "When you are working on something and get confused or upset, you need to ask for help. When you ask for help you need to call Ms. Smith, and say, 'I need help.'"

   Have the child describe the social skill.

   Ask the child, "What do you do when you need help?"

   Child states what to do when he needs help.

   Say: "Right, I call Ms. Smith and say, 'I need help.'"

2. **Model with the child.**

   "Watch me: I am going to show you how to ask for help."

   Have the child tell you if you asked for help.

   Ask, "Did I ask for help?

   Child answers, "Yes."

   Say, "Right! I called Ms. Smith and said, 'I need help.'"

3. **The child models with you.**

   "Show me how you ask for help." Child models with you.

   Say, "Good, you called Ms. Smith and said, 'I need help.'"

4. **Give an example of the social skill by modeling it appropriately and ask the child if you asked for help.**

   Then ask, "What did I do?"

   The child states what you did.

5. **The child demonstrates the skill appropriately.**

   Say, "Show me how to ask for help." (Child demonstrates.)

   Say, "Great! You called Ms. Smith and said, 'I need help.'"

Keys to Effective Classroom Management

♦ When tasks are developmentally appropriate, children are more likely to be successful and independent.

♦ Transfer of learning

   ♦ When beginning an activity that is difficult for a specific child, remind him to ask for help if he needs it.

   ♦ Send a note home to parents (see sample on the next page) explaining the social skill that you are teaching the children.

Dear Parents:

This week your child is working on the social skill of asking for help. If you remind your child to use this skill at home it will help us at school.

This is what your child is learning:

When I need help:

1. I call my teacher's name or call my parents (mommy, daddy).
2. I say, "I need help."

When your child needs help, give him or her a chance to ask you to help. Please affirm your child when he or she asks for help and give your child the needed assistance.

Thanks so much!

Sincerely,

_____

Asking Permission

The Issue

When learning to work with a group, children need to learn boundaries. There are some things that are appropriate at home but not at school. For example, you can go to the restroom whenever you want to at home, but at school there are times when you need to ask.

Overview

Asking permission is a life-long requirement. Children who learn that they need to ask permission learn to respect authority—and they learn when they need to ask, and when they can go ahead and act independently.

Goal

♦ To teach children when to ask permission before doing things in school

Solutions

Consider the following suggested script:

1. **Describe the social skill.**

    Say, "When I ask permission, I call my teacher's name and say, 'May I go play in centers?' or 'May I go to the restroom?'"

    Have the child describe social skill.

    Ask the child, "What do I do when I want to go play in centers?"

    The child states what you do when you want to play in centers.

    Say, "Right, you call your teacher's name (Ms. Smith) and say, 'May I play in centers now?'"

2. **Model the behavior with the child.**

    "Watch me. I am going to show you how to ask permission."

    Have child tell if you asked permission.

    Ask, "Did I call the teacher's name and say, 'May I play in centers now'?" Child answers, "Yes."

    Say, "Right! I said, 'Ms. Smith, may I play in centers now?'"

3. **The child models with you.**

    "Show me how you ask permission." Child models with you.

    Say, "Yes, you said 'Ms. Smith, may I play in centers now?'"

4. **Give an example of the social skill by modeling it correctly.**

    Then ask, "What did I do?"

    The child states what you did.

5. **The child demonstrates how to ask for permission.**

    Say, "Show me how to ask permission to play with the cars."

    (Child demonstrates.)

    Say, "Great! You called my name and said, 'May I play with the cars?'"

6. **Practice asking permission to do other things on the next day.**

Keys to Effective Classroom Management

♦ Children need to ask permission to do something so that they can learn to respect authority. That does not always mean that the answer will be "Yes." Always thank the child for asking. If you are not sure about something, you can always answer, "Let me think about it" or "We'll see." These answers also help children to learn to wait, defer gratification, and learn self-control.

♦ Transfer of learning:

    ♦ Remind the child to ask permission before he does specific things in the classroom.

    ♦ Send a note home to parents (see sample on the next page) explaining the social skill that you are teaching the children.

Dear Parents:

This week your child is working on the social skill of asking permission. If you remind your child to use this skill at home it will help us at school.

This is what your child is learning about asking permission:

1. I call my teacher's name (or your mommy or daddy's name).
2. I say, "May I _____, please (go outside, get a drink)?"

Please acknowledge your child when he or she asks permission.

Thanks so much!

Sincerely,

_____

Asking for a Toy

The Issue

Preschoolers may not have had the opportunity to learn to ask others when they want a specific item. At school they have to learn to share, and they also need to learn to assert themselves in a positive manner. Although asking for a toy is related to sharing (giving possessions to others) and turn-taking (waiting and responding in a specific order), asking another child for a toy is different in several respects: 1) the child must initiate the request; 2) the child must communicate expressively; and 3) the response to the child's communication depends on the other child. Teaching children to ask for toys is one way that you can prevent "bullying" in your classroom.

Overview

When children learn to ask for a toy that they would like to play with, they are learning to assert themselves to get their needs met. As children learn to ask, they are less likely to grab toys and start fights in the classroom.

Goal

◆ To teach children to ask for a toy that a peer is playing with rather than grab it

Solutions

Consider the following suggested script:

1. **Describe the social skill.**

   Say, "When I want to play with a toy that my friend has, I say, 'May I play with the car, please?' I wait until she finished playing with it."

   Have the child describe the social skill.

   Ask the child, "What do I do when I want to play with a car that my friend is playing with?"

   Child states what you do when you want to play with the car.

   Say, "Right, I ask to play with the car and I wait for my friend to finish."

2. **Model with the child.**

   "Watch me. I am going to show you how to ask to play with the cars."

   Have the child tell if you asked to play with the cars in the right way.

   Ask, "Did I ask to play with the cars and wait for my friend to finish?"

   Child answers, "Yes."

   Say, "Right! I asked to play with the cars and waited for my friend to finish."

3. **The child models with you.**

   "Show me how you ask to play with a toy that your friend is playing with."

   The child models with you.

   Say, "Yes, you asked to play with the cars and you waited for your friend to finish."

4. **Give an example of social skill by modeling it with a peer and ask the child if you asked to play with the toy in the right way.**

   Then ask, "What did I do?"

   The child states what you did.

5. **The child demonstrates with a peer.**

   Say, "Show me how you ask to play with the trucks."

   Say, "Great! You said, 'May I play with the trucks?' and you waited for your friend to finish playing."

Keys to Effective Classroom Management

◆ Asking is only the first step. The other child may say "no." In that case the child needs to be reminded that his friend has not finished playing with the toy. You can ask the friend when he will be finished with the toy—and ask him to give the toy to the other child when he is finished.

203

Dear Parents:

This week your child is working on the social skill of asking for a toy that another child is using. If you remind your child to do this at home it will help us at school.

This is what your child is learning. When he or she wants a toy that someone is playing with:

1. Your child says, "May I play with the _____, please?" (doll, car)
2. He or she waits until the friend is finished playing with the toy.
3. Your child thanks the friend when he or she gives your child the toy.

Please acknowledge your child when he or she asks to play with a toy, rather than grabbing it away!

Thanks so much!

Sincerely,

_____

The publisher grants permission for this page to be photocopied for classroom use only.

© Gryphon House, Inc. 800-638-0928. www.gryphonhouse.com

The Issue

Teaching children to invite others to play improves social interaction in the classroom and builds the child's repertoire of social skills. It is similar to the skill of "Getting Started in Play" on pages 164-165. The skill presented in that chapter required the child simply to hand a peer a toy and say, "Let's play." The script presented here requires the child to initiate a specific joint activity. With some children you may be able to use the suggestions on pages 90-91, "Learning How to Become Part of a Play Setting." The script below shows how you, as the teacher, can specifically teach children with social difficulties how to initiate an activity with their friends.

Overview

Many children do not know how to initiate play with peers. They may be used to playing by themselves or having older siblings that initiate play at home. When you teach children to start play activities you are building potential leadership skills.

Goal

◆ To teach children how to invite peers to play

Solutions

Consider the following suggested script:

1. **Describe the social skill.**
   Say, "When we want to play with our friends, we think of a something fun to do, and we say to our friend, 'Come on, let's play ___ (ball).'"
   Have the child describe the social skill.
   Ask the child, "What do I do when I want to play with my friends?"
   The child states what to do when he wants to play with his friends.
   Say, "Right, I think of something fun to do and say, 'Come on, let's play (ball).'"

2. **Model with the child.**
   "Watch me. I am going to show you how to invite Heather to play." (demonstrate)
   Have the child tell if you invited Heather to play.
   Ask, "Did I think of something fun to do and say, 'Let's play dolls?'"
   Child answers, "Yes."
   Say, "Right! I thought of something fun to do and said to Heather, 'Let's play dolls.'"

3. **The child models with you.**
   "Show me how you invite Justin to play."
   Child models with you.
   Say, "Good, you thought of something fun to do and said, 'Come on, let's cook.'"

4. **Give an example of the social skill by modeling it with a peer and ask the child if you invited Quentin to play.**
   Then ask, "What did I do?"
   The child states what you did.

5. **The child demonstrates with a peer.**
   Say, "Show me how to invite Quentin to play."
   (Child demonstrates with peer.)
   Say, "Great! You thought of something fun to do and said, 'Come on, let's play trucks'."

Keys to Effective Classroom Management

◆ Two children may not want to play with the same toys. When this happens, explain to the child that he may need to ask his friend what he wants to play with.

Dear Parents:

This week your child is working on the social skill of inviting a friend to play. If you remind your child to use this skill at home it will help us at school.

This is what your child is learning about inviting a friend to play. When he or she wants to invite a friend to play:

1. Your child thinks of something fun to do.
2. Then he or she says to the friend, "Come on—let's play _____" (dolls, cars, ball, and so on).

Please acknowledge your child when he or she invites a friend to play.

Thanks so much!

Sincerely,

_____

Asking for an Alternative Activity

The Issue

When children become frustrated in one activity, they need to learn how to ask for an alternative activity or to ask for a break.

Overview

Adults generally know when to stop and take a break, then finish the frustrating task later. Asking for a break, or asking to do something else, enables the child to gain self-control. Instead of throwing a tantrum, destroying materials, or other negative behavior, the child can be prompted to ask to do something else or to take a break. This method is one of several ways of dealing with negative behavior that has the pay-off of escaping tasks.

Goal

♦ To help children recognize that when they become frustrated with an activity that they can ask to take a break or do something different

Solutions

Consider the following:

♦ Determine that the negative behavior has the purpose of escaping a low-preference task.

♦ Make sure that the task is developmentally appropriate and has value to the child's growth as a member of the school community. If the task is not important for the child, then it may not be the time to address it.

♦ Determine how long the child will work on the low-preference task, such as sitting for a short time during Circle Time or for table toy activities.

♦ Observe the child while he is engaged in the task. What behaviors indicate that he is getting tired and may demonstrate negative behavior?

♦ Before the child demonstrates negative behavior, prompt the child to ask for a break or to ask to do something else.

  ♦ Ask the child, "Do you need a break?"

  ♦ If the child nods or says, "yes," tell him to say, "I need a break."

  ♦ When the child asks for a break, remove the low-preference task and take a trip to the water fountain or the restroom.

♦ Use a similar procedure for asking for an alternative activity. You can show the child two objects and ask if he would like to do something else for a while.

Keys to Effective Classroom Management

♦ Be sure that classroom tasks are developmentally appropriate for the children in your classroom. If children refuse tasks, ask yourself if they are important. If a task is important (such as picking up toys or sitting still at lunchtime), then use this strategy of prompting the child to ask for an alternative or a break. The child can finish the low-preference task later. Make sure that you praise the child for his good work. You want to help the child to build his ability to complete tasks.

207

Nonverbal Communication

The Issue

Children may not know how to interpret other people's nonverbal communication. When they learn to interpret what others are saying with their bodies, they are better able to interact in socially appropriate ways.

Overview

Appropriate behavior involves reading subtle messages from others. By recognizing nonverbal communication, children are better able to express feelings and develop empathy for others.

Goal

◆ To teach children to recognize the meaning of body language

Solutions

The following ideas will help you teach children the important skill of interpreting nonverbal communication.

◆ Develop a file of pictures of children and adults with actions and body postures that demonstrate strong feelings. Examples of these include a mother with her hands on her hips, a father smiling with one hand going up in the air, a teacher smiling, and a boy with a downcast expression as a peer grabs a toy. A number of language kits have excellent pictures such as these.

◆ In the learning circle, ask the children to tell you about the picture.
  ◆ What is happening in the picture?
  ◆ What is the child (person) saying?
  ◆ How does the child (person) feel?
  ◆ Why do you think that the child (person) feels ___?
  ◆ What are some things that make you feel ___?

◆ Ask other members of the class to tell when they feel ___.

◆ Have children show with their faces how to look ___.

◆ Ask children individually to show what the person in the picture is doing and feeling. You may need to demonstrate this to the class at first.

Keys to Effective Classroom Management

◆ For some children, you may have to conduct these lessons in small groups or individually. Exaggerate your actions and facial expression during these lessons.

Tone of Voice

The Issue

Young children often do not recognize that their tone of voice communicates information, positive or negative, to others. When taught to discriminate various tones of voice, children learn that the tone of voice that they use impacts the feelings and attitudes of others.

Overview

Because the tone of voice that children use is so powerful in affecting the responses of others, you need to teach children to recognize differences in their tones of their voice. Children also need to acknowledge how the way something is said makes them feel. Many young children may not know how to use their "polite voices" unless specifically taught in the classroom.

Goals

◆ To teach children to distinguish various tones of voice so they can recognize how they make the listener feel when he hears them

◆ To teach children to use their polite voices with peers and teachers in the classroom

Solutions

Consider the following steps:

1. Begin at Circle Time with a role play of a typical child interaction, such as asking for a toy.
2. Explain that you are going to ask Johnny for the truck by saying, "I want the truck."
3. Explain that you need to ask Johnny using a polite voice. Exaggerate your intonation using positive facial expression.
4. Demonstrate the use of a various voices.
5. Role-play by saying to various children in the circle, "I want the truck (or car, bear, etc.)." Use various tones of voices.
6. Ask children how it makes them feel when you use a polite voice.
7. Ask children how it makes them feel when you use other tones of voice.
8. Ask children if the tone of voice makes them want to share with you.
9. Role-play the use of a polite voice with puppets, dolls, or stuffed animals.
10. Ask the children to say whether the puppet used a polite voice.
11. Have children demonstrate asking you for a toy using polite voices.
12. Explain how the polite voice makes you want to share.
13. Have children role play using polite voices with their peers.
14. Explain that even when using a polite voice, some friends may not be ready to share the toy yet. That is okay. If we wait, our friends usually will be ready to share later when they are finished playing with the toy.

Keys to Effective Classroom Management

◆ The goal in this lesson is to teach children to use their polite voices with others. Before activities such as centers or recess, remind children to use their polite voices when they are talking to their friends. Some children will need to be reminded individually. Letting parents know that you are teaching children about using polite voices in a note or newsletter helps them to work on the same skill at home. This promotes transfer of learning. You can hang posters or pictures in the classroom that can be associated with using a polite voice. Explain that the person in the picture is using a polite voice. This also serves as a reminder to the children to use their polite voices.

Facial Expressions

The Issue

Children who can interpret the expressions of others can adjust their behavior in response to others.

Overview

Labeling emotions, expressing emotions, and nonverbal communication have an impact on behavior. Facial expressions convey important social information.

Goal

◆ To teach children to identify, demonstrate, and give a reason for specific feelings

Solutions

Consider the following steps:

1. While sitting in the learning circle, explain that the class is going to play a game of "Guess How I Feel."
2. When you show a facial expression, the child raises his hand when he knows how you are feeling.
3. Talk about several types of expressions and demonstrate a facial expression with each: happy, sad, angry, hurt, confused, surprised, bored, tired, sick, and so on.
4. Demonstrate an expression.
5. Call on a child to identify the feeling.
6. Talk about why someone might feel that way.
7. Have the child who guessed the feeling be the next one to demonstrate a feeling in front of the circle.
8. Help the children to identify the feeling. Have the child in front tell when he feels _____.
9. Other children have their turns to demonstrate facial expressions.

Keys to Effective Classroom Management

◆ The number and types of facial expressions depends on the development of the children in the group. Most groups of preschoolers will have children with a range of levels of development. Show one difficult expression after a few easier expressions to identify.

Body Language

The Issue

Children need to learn to recognize that their actions and the actions of others have a message.

Overview

Actions speak louder than words. When children are better able to read body language, they can adjust their actions in response to the message.

Goal

◆ To teach children to identify and express messages via body language

Solutions

Consider the following steps:

1. In the learning circle, explain to the children that they talk with their mouths and with their bodies.

2. Show pictures from your picture file or from a language development kit that show good examples of body language. Talk about what the person is saying with his body.

3. Model what the person in the picture is doing and ask the children what you are saying with your body.

4. Ask the children, as a group, to show what the person in the picture is doing.

5. Ask the children why they think that the person is doing that.

6. Have the children take turns in front of the class. Give the child a picture and have him show the class what the person is doing in the picture. Remind the child to talk only with his body, not with his mouth.

7. Ask the class what the child is saying with his body.

Keys to Effective Classroom Management

◆ Different children are able to understand body language at different levels. Give the children with less understanding of this area the easier pictures to demonstrate.

211

Sign Language and Gestures

The Issue

Many children with the most difficult behaviors lack the ability to express themselves verbally. Some children are not developmentally able to produce speech to the extent that they need it to make their wants and needs known in the classroom. In these instances, you can teach the child to make his needs known through gestures or simple sign language.

Overview

Any number of problems can interfere with the child's ability to express himself verbally: developmental delays, delayed language, physical disabilities, or emotional problems. Research shows that the use of sign language and nonverbal communication is not a "crutch." Quite the opposite, these forms of communication promote speech and language development.

Goal

◆ To teach children to communicate basic wants and needs via gestures or basic signs

Solutions

Consider the following steps:

1. Observe the child with the problem behavior during the day to determine when and under what circumstances the problem behavior occurs.
2. What is the message that the child's behavior communicates? Some common messages are:

   ◆ I want a break!   ◆ I'm finished!

   ◆ I want ___!   ◆ Stay away!

   ◆ I'm mad!   ◆ Look at me!

3. Is there a gesture to communicate the message? For example, "I want ___" may be expressed through pointing. This gesture is certainly better than grabbing or throwing a tantrum!
4. If there is not a gesture, a simple manual sign may be appropriate such as the sign for "finished" or "break."
5. Teach the child the sign or gesture through role-playing.
6. Prompt the child to use the sign during the day, before the negative behavior occurs.
7. Make sure that others in the classroom know the gesture or sign.
8. Affirm the child with the problem behavior when he uses the sign or gesture.

Keys to Effective Classroom Management

◆ Signs or gestures will not interfere with the child's ability to learn to express herself verbally. It will, however, improve the ability to interact in the classroom and express wants and needs. Pair the sign or gesture with your communication to the children on a regular basis so that you are modeling this method of expression. As the child is able to communicate through signs and gestures, encourage vocalization and words as well. Maintain a light and positive attitude if you expect the child to respond.

Communication to Enhance Acceptance

The Issue

One of the greatest human needs is acceptance. Maslow's Hierarchy puts the "Need for Affiliation" high on the ladder of basic human needs (Morrison, 2004). Children want to be accepted by others but may lack the ability or skills they need to engage in socially accepted behavior.

Overview

Communication behaviors, verbal and nonverbal, all enhance social acceptance. When you model and teach these behaviors, it helps children learn ways to become an accepted member of the learning community.

Goals

◆ To teach children behaviors to promote social acceptance because they see these behaviors modeled by you and their peers

◆ To help children experience social success in the classroom, which they are likely to transfer these behaviors to other places

Solutions

The following communication behaviors are learned through modeling:

◆ Smiling

◆ Using a positive tone of voice

◆ Eye contact

◆ Getting attention through proximity before talking

◆ Gentle touch for people and pets

The following communication behaviors may need to be taught directly:

◆ Calling peers by name

◆ Giving compliments

◆ Saying "please" and "thank you"

◆ Inviting friends to play

Keys to Effective Classroom Management

◆ Most children learn behaviors to promote social acceptance from observing others in the environment. Some children have had negative role models and must be taught behaviors to help them to become an active and accepted group member. Other children have developmental problems that may interfere with their ability to interact socially. You can teach them alternative skills and structure the classroom to become more accepting of others.

Putting It Into Practice: Oliver

The principles supporting this narrative are:

- Classroom management requires teachers to deal with individual problems.
- When one technique fails, try another.
- Some children respond quickly, while others require a longer time to respond.
- Involve the family as much as possible when dealing with a child's problems.
- Sharing personal experiences will facilitate children's understanding of their own problems.
- Children may need instruction about expressing their feelings before they can verbalize their needs and concerns.
- Professional assistance beyond the classroom is necessary on occasion.
- Patience and good humor are essential to success.

"No, it's not," screamed Oliver. This was a frequent cry of Oliver, along with "No," "I don't want to," and "You can't make me." Martha, the teacher of the four-year-old class, was exasperated with Oliver. Regardless of how she tried to reward Oliver, he would not follow rules or routines. Lately he had begun bargaining with her, and she realized that she was falling into a trap. When asked to do something, Oliver would ask if he could go to centers if he did as asked. Rather than the teacher setting the standard, Oliver was in charge.

Martha realized that she spent much of her time disciplining Oliver and that his behavior limited the progress of other children in the classroom. Sending Oliver to the "thinking chair" was a struggle, and someone had to monitor him to keep him in the chair. Trips to the thinking chair were more frequent and his behavior was deteriorating. When Oliver's mother was called to come get him, she came to the school in tears. Oliver's father had left her with two preschoolers and no one knew where he was. She was working at a minimum wage job and would not be paid for the hours that she was unable to work because of Oliver's behavior.

Martha set up a conference with Ms. Rice, Oliver's mother, on her day off. She realized that his mother struggled with depression, the responsibility of two preschoolers, and financial problems after the father had abandoned them. She had no family and few friends to help her. The mother stated that the love of her two boys was what kept her going every day, and that she would help Oliver in any way possible.

Martha observed Oliver at school and recorded his negative behaviors for a week. She realized that his negative behaviors and refusal to work provided him plenty of individual attention. Also, it seemed that Oliver had a desire to control the actions in the classroom. She knew from her parent conference that Oliver had received little attention at home except for when he behaved inappropriately. Then he received negative attention. For Oliver, negative attention from adults was what he was used to—and he seemed to enjoy negative adult attention. Martha also watched what Oliver did during his unstructured time so that she would know what his preferences were.

After thinking about what she had observed in Oliver and what she had learned from the parent conference, Martha developed a plan. The first

thing that she realized was that Oliver really was a sad little boy. Rather than giving commands, she recognized that she needed to become more animated in her instructions in an effort to make learning fun and exciting. She realized that her tone of voice and facial expressions must be positive and pleasant if she expected Oliver to cooperate with her.

Next, she decided to give Oliver choices, such as the choice of crayons or pencils, the choice of the red mat or the blue mat, and the choice of whether to stand near the back of the line or the front. Whenever she wanted Oliver to do something, she gave him choices. However, she realized that the choices had to be developmentally appropriate and limited to two items. Additionally, Martha gave Oliver a choice of classroom jobs, which provided him plenty of positive attention from her and his peers.

Martha knew that Oliver was reluctant to attempt new classroom tasks. She decided that she would use several strategies. First, she used a high-probability request sequence where she embedded new skills within familiar skills so that he could experience success in a non-threatening context. She also used the collaborative task format: You do the first one and I will do the second one; you do the first three and I will do the next one. And she applied "Grandma's Rule": When you finish your work, then you can go to centers. Martha recognized the fact that "Grandma's Rule" (see page 184) was different from Oliver's bargaining (where he specified the reward and conditions) or bribery (a payoff for something illegal or harmful). This did take extra time, but it was far less time-consuming than dealing with Oliver's negative behavior. Also, these strategies seemed to help some of the other children as well.

The final action that Martha took was to give Oliver plenty of positive attention when he came into the classroom at the beginning of the day. She realized that if he had attention for positive actions early in his day, that he would not be so deprived of attention that he would resort to negative behavior to obtain it. With all of these actions, Oliver made excellent progress. There were still difficult days. On these days, Martha communicated with Ms. Rice. She learned that Oliver's father was sometimes taking the boys for visits. On some days, Oliver had stayed up late the night before or had experienced a disappointment at home. On other days, the answer was right before Martha's eyes in the classroom. An altercation with a classmate early in the day could set the stage for Oliver's negative moods. Martha realized that Oliver's negative responses still

(continued on the next page)

occurred, but with far less frequency. With her positive attitude, her teaching strategies, and communication with his mother, she no longer got into power struggles with Oliver. She knew that Oliver would be a child that she would never forget—he had taught her many things about children and about herself.

Resources

Books

Axline, V. 1981. *Play therapy (reissue edition)*. New York: Ballantine Books.

Beaty, J. 1998. *Prosocial guidance for the preschool child*. Columbus, OH: Prentice Hall.

Berk, L. & A. Winsler. 1995. *Scaffolding children's learning: Vygotsky and early childhood education*. Washington, DC: National Association for the Education of Young Children.

Charles, C. 2000. *The synergetic classroom: Joyful teaching and gentle discipline*. New York: Addison Wesley Longman, Inc.

Close, N. 2001. *Listening to children: Talking with children about difficult issues*. Boston: Allyn & Bacon.

Diffily, D. & K. Morrison, Eds. 1996. *Family-friendly communication for early childhood programs*. Washington, DC: National Association for the Education of Young Children.

Dill, V.S. 1998. *A peaceable school*. Bloomington, IN: Phi Delta Kappa.

Greenberg, P. 1991. *Character development: Encouraging self-esteem & self-discipline in infants, toddlers, & two-year-olds*. Washington, DC: National Association for the Education of Young Children.

Greenman, J. 2001. *What happened to the world? Helping children cope in turbulent times*. Watertown, MA: Bright Horizons Family Solutions.

Hemmeter, M.L., G.E. Joseph, B.J. Smith, & S. Sandall, Eds. 2001. *DEC recommended practices in program assessment*. Longmont, CO: Sopris West.

Hundert, J. 1995. *Enhancing social competence in young students: School-based approaches*. Austin, TX: Pro-Ed.

Kaiser, B. & J.S. Rasminsky. 1999. *Meeting the challenge: Effective strategies for challenging behaviours in early childhood environments*. Ottawa, Ontario: Canadian Child Care Federation.

Marion, M. 2002. *Guidance of young children, sixth edition*. Columbus, OH: Merrill.

McCracken, J.B. 1987. *Reducing stress in young children's lives.* Washington, DC: National Association for the Education of Young Children.

McCracken, J.B. 1993. *Valuing diversity: The primary years.* Washington, DC: National Association for the Education of Young Children.

Neugebauer, B., Ed. 1992. *Alike and different, exploring our humanity with young children, revised edition.* Redmond, WA: Childcare Information Exchange.

Katz, L. & D. McClellan. 1991. *The teacher's role in the social development of young children.* Urbana, IL: Clearinghouse on Elementary and Early Childhood Education.

Powell, R., H.J. McLaughlin, T. Savage, & S. Zehm. 2000. *Classroom management: Perspectives on the social curriculum.* New York: Prentice Hall.

Reynolds, E. 2001. *Guiding young children, third edition.* Mountain View, CA: Mayfield Publishing Company.

Sandall, S. & M. Ostrosky, Eds. 1999. *Young exceptional children: Practical ideas for addressing challenging behaviors.* Missoula, MT: The Division for Early Childhood of the Council for Exceptional Children.

Sandall, S. & M. Ostrosky, Eds. 2000. *Natural environments and inclusion.* Longmont, CO: Sopris West.

Sandall, S. & M. Ostrosky, Eds. 2001. *Teaching strategies: What to do to support young children's development.* Missoula, MT: The Division for Early Childhood of the Council for Exceptional Children.

Schiller, P. 1999. *Start smart! Building brain power in the early years.* Beltsville, MD: Gryphon House.

Simon, S. & S. Olds. 1977. *Helping your child learn right from wrong: A guide to values clarification.* New York: McGraw-Hill.

Slaby, R., W. Roedell, D. Arezzo, & K. Hendrix. 1995. *Early violence prevention: Tools for teachers of young children.* Washington, DC: National Association for the Education of Young Children.

Sparzo, F. 1999. *The ABC's of behavior change.* Bloomington, IN: Phi Delta Kappa.

Stone, J.G. 2001. *Building classroom community: The early childhood teacher's role.* Washington, DC: National Association for the Education of Young Children.

Wolery, M. & J. Wilbers, Eds. 1994. *Including children with special needs in early childhood programs.* Washington, DC: National Association for the Education of Young Children.

Wolfgang, C. 2001. *Solving discipline and classroom management problems, methods and models for today's teachers, 5th edition.* New York: John Wiley & Sons.

Children's Books

Books About the Body

Aliki. 1989. *My five senses.* New York: HarperTrophy.

Balestrino, P. 1989. *The skeleton inside you.* New York: HarperTrophy.

Cole, J. 1990. *The magic school bus: Inside the human body.* New York: Scholastic.

Ingoglia, G. 1998. *Look inside your body: A poke and look learning book.* New York: Grosset & Dunlap.

Kagan, N. 1999. *What is a bellybutton?: First questions and answers about the human body.* New York: Time Life, Inc.

Showers, P. 1997. *Sleep is for everyone.* New York: HarperTrophy.

Showers, P. 1991. *Your skin and mine.* New York: HarperCollins.

Books About Communication

Bennett, P. 1995. *Communicating nature's secrets.* New York: Thompson Learning.

Castle, S. 1977. *Face talk, hand talk, body talk.* Garden City: Doubleday.

Otto, C. 1994. *I can tell by touching.* New York: HarperCollins.

Pfeffer, W. 1999. *Sounds all around.* New York: HarperCollins.

Rau, D.M. 1998. *The secret code.* New York: Children's Press.

Books About Death

Buscaglia, L. 1983. *The fall of freddy the leaf.* New York: Holt, Rinehart, and Winston.

Viorst, J. 1971. *The tenth good thing about Barney.* Hartford: Atheneum.

Books About Feelings

Aliki. 1984. *Feelings.* New York: Greenwillow Books.

Atkinson, M. 1997. *Why can't I be happy all the time?: Questions children ask about feelings.* New York: DK Publications.

Bergstrom, C. 1980. *Losing your best friend.* New York: Human Sciences Press.

Berry, J. 1996. *Feeling sad.* New York: Scholastic.

Bonsall, C. 1964. *It's mine! A greedy book.* New York: HarperCollins.

Braithwaite, A. 1998. *Feeling scared.* Milwaukee: Gareth Stevens Publications.

Crary, E. 1992. *I'm mad.* Seattle: Parenting Press.

Fannelli, S. 1995. *My map book.* New York: HarperCollins.

LeShan, E. 1972. *What makes me feel this way? Growing up with human emotions.* New York: MacMillan.

Books About Friends

Aliki. 1995. *Best friends together again.* New York: Greenwillow Books.

Berenstain, S. & J. Berenstain. 1987. *The Berenstain Bears and the trouble with friends.* New York: Random House.

Brown, L. & M. Brown. 1998. *How to be a friend.* Boston: Little, Brown and Company.

Carle, E. 1995. *Do you want to be my friend?* New York: HarperCollins.

Cohen, M. 1989. *Will I have a friend?* New York: Aladdin Library.

Cohn, J. 1987. *I had a friend named Peter.* New York: William Morrow and Company.

Gomi, T. 1995. *My friends.* New York: Chronicle Books.

Hallinan, P. 1989. *My teacher's my friend.* Nashville: Ideals Children's Books.

Hoff, S. 1985. *Who will be my friends?* New York: HarperCollins.

Krasny, L. 2001. *How to be a friend.* Madison: Turtleback Books.

Milne, A. 1997. *Winnie the Pooh's friendship tales.* New York: Penguin Putnam.

Lindman, M. 1995. *Flicka, Ricka, Dicka, and their new friend.* Illinois: Albert Whitman & Company.

Lyon, G. 1993. *Together.* New York: Orchard Books.

Mayer, M. 2001. *Just my friend and me (reissue edition).* New York: Golden Books.

Pfister, M. 1992. *The rainbow fish.* New York: North-South Books.

Satin, A. 1998. *Biscuit finds a friend.* New York: HarperCollins.

Books About Homes

Barrett, J. 1998. *Old MacDonald had an apartment house.* New York: Atheneum.

Barton, B. 1981. *Building a house.* New York: William Morrow.

Berenstain, J. & S. Berenstain. 1983. *The Berenstain Bears and the messy room.* New York: Random House.

Burton, V. 1978. *The little house.* Boston, MA. Houghton Mifflin.

Carle, Eric. 1991. *A house for hermit crab.* New York: Simon and Schuster.

Chessen, B. 1998. *Animal homes.* New York: Scholastic.

Chessen, B. 1998. *Where do birds live?* New York: Scholastic.

Connelly, L. 1996. *Mr. Noisy builds a house.* Santa Barbara: Creative Teaching Press.

Cutts, D. 1979. *The house that jack built.* Mahwah, NJ: Troll Books.

Dorros, A. 1992. *This is my house.* New York: Scholastic Inc.

Hoberman, M. 1978. *A house is a house for me.* New York: Scholastic.

Jeunesse, G. 1995. *Houses.* New York: Scholastic.

Morris, A. 1992. *Houses and homes.* New York: Mulberry Books.

Williams, R. 1994. *Who lives here?* Santa Barbara: Creative Teaching Press.

Books About Neighborhoods

Brett, J. 2003. *Town mouse, country mouse.* New York: Puffin.

Brandenberg, F. 1977. *Nice new neighbors.* New York: Greenwillow Books.

Komaiko, L. 1990. *My perfect neighborhood.* New York: HarperCollins.

Prather, R. 1970. *New neighbors.* New York: McGraw-Hill.

Prelutsky, J. 1984. *New kid on the block.* New York: Greenwillow Books.

Raskin, E. 1989. *Nothing ever happens on my block.* New York: Aladdin Books.

Robbins, K. 1985. *City/country.* New York: Viking.

Books About Cultures

Aardema, V. 1979. *Half-a-ball-of-kenki: An Ashanti tale retold.* New York: Viking.

Cannon, J. 1993. *Stellaluna.* San Diego: Harcourt.

Chin-Lee, C. 1993. *Almond cookies and dragon well tea.* Chicago: Polychrome Publishing Corporation.

Cowan-Fletcher, J.1994. *It takes a village.* New York: Scholastic.

Furchgott, T. 1983. *Nanda in India.* New York: Dutton.

French, V., & R. Collins. 2002. *Write around the world.* Oxford: Oxford UP.

Gray, N. 1991. *A country far away.* New York: Orchard Books.

Hallinan, P.K. 2002. *A rainbow of friends.* Nashville: Ideals Children's Books.

McDermott, G. 1988. *Anansi the spider: A tale from the Ashanti.* New York: Henry Holt.

Paulsen, G. 1995. *La tortilleria.* New York: Harcourt.

Sweeney, J. 1996. *Me on the map.* New York: Random House.

Viorst, J. 1989. *Alexander y el dia terrible, horrible, espantoso, horroroso.* New York: Aladdin.

Books About School

Ahlberg, A. & J. Ahlberg. 1990. *Starting school.* New York: Puffin.

Baer, E. 1992. *This is the way we go to school.* New York: Scholastic.

Berenstain, S. & J. Berenstain. 1978. *The Berenstain Bears go to school.* New York: Random House.

Hains, H. 1992. *My new school.* New York: Penguin.

Wildes, I. 1956. *The giraffe who went to school.* New York: T.S. Denison and Company.

Books About Self-Concept

Bailey, C.S. 1978. *The little rabbit who wanted red wings.* New York: Platt & Munk.

DeLuise, D. 1990. *Charlie the caterpillar.* New York: Simon and Schuster.

Hoffman, M. 1991. *Amazing grace.* New York: Dial Books for Young Readers.

Krause, L. 1978. *Leo the late bloomer.* New York: Scholastic.

Lionni, L. 1973. *Swimmy.* New York: Knopf Children's Paperbacks.

Books About Solving Problems

Barasch, L. 2000. *Radio rescue.* New York: Frances Foster Book.

Tarlton, J. 1986. *Danny's dilemma.* New Zealand: Ashton Scholastic Limited.

Viorst, J. 1982. *Alexander and the terrible, horrible, no good, very bad day.* New York: Atheneum.

Miscellaneous Books

Andrews, J. 2002. *Very last first time.* New York: Groundwood Douglas.

Berenstain, S. & J. Berenstain. 1981. *The Berenstain Bears forget their manners.* New York: Random House.

Bernhard, E. 1996. *A ride on mother's back.* New York: Harcourt.

Brett, J. 1996. *The mitten.* New York: Putnam.

Brown, A. 1998. *Voices in the park.* New York: DK Publication.

Brown, M. 1982. *Goodnight moon.* New York: HarperCollins.

Carr, J. 1995. *Dark day. Light night.* New York: Hyperion.

Cohen, M. 1977. *When will I read?* New York: Greenwillow Books.

DePaola, T. 1978. *Pancakes for breakfast.* New York: Harcourt, Brace & Javonovich.

Flack, M. 1932. *Ask Mr. Bear.* New York: Collier Books.

Gibbons, G. 1993. *Puff-flash-bang!* New York: William Morrow & Co.

Kraus, R. 1986. *Where are you going, little mouse?* New York: Mulberry Books.

Mayer, M. 1989. *There's a nightmare in my closet.* New York: New York Publishing Co.

Pfister, M. 1992. *The rainbow fish.* New York: North South Books.

Quinsey, M. 1986. *Why does that man have such a big nose?* Seattle: Parenting Press.

Rabe, B. 1988. *The balancing girl.* New York: Demco Media.

Rockwell, A. 1985. *In our house.* New York: HarperCollins.

Samoyault, T. 1997. *Give me a sign!* New York: Viking Penguin.

Sawicki, N. 1990. *The little red house.* New York: Shepard Books.

Sharratt, N. 1992. *I look like this.* Cambridge: Candlewick Press.

Shriver, M. 2001. *What's wrong with Timmy?* Boston: Little Brown and Company.

Simon, N. 1993. *Why am I different?* New York: Albert Whitman and Co.

Spier, P. 1993. *Fox went out on a chilly night.* Garden City: Doubleday Dell.

Wood, D. 2001. *Old turtle.* New York: Scholastic.

Zutter, H. & S. MacDonald. 1997. *Who says dogs go bow-wow?* New York: Picture Yearling.

Videos

Caring and Learning, by Laura Colker. Teaching Strategies, Inc. 1991. 800.637.3652.

Developmentally Appropriate Practice: Children Ages Birth Through Five Years, #854, National Association for the Education of Young Children. 1991. 800.424.2460.

Developmentally Appropriate Practice: Curriculum - The Role of the Teacher, #856, National Association for the Education of Young Children. 1992. 800.424.2460.

How Are Kids Smart? Multiple Intelligences in the Classroom, National Professional Resources, Inc. 1995. 800.453.7461.

Preschoolers: Social & Emotional Development, The Developing Child Series. Magna Systems. 1994. 95 West County Line Road, Barrington, IL 60010.

Ten Things Every Child Needs, Robert B. McCormick Tribune Foundation, Chicago, IL. 1997. www.amazon.com. 1997.

Room Arrangement as a Teaching Strategy, by Diane Trister Dodge and Bonnie Kittredge. Teaching Strategies, Inc. 2003. 800.637.3652.

Toddlerhood: Physical & Cognitive Development, The Developing Child Series. Magna Systems. 2003. 95 West County Line Road, Barrington, IL 60010.

Organizations

Association for Childhood Education International
17904 Georgia Avenue, Suite 215
Olney, MD 20832
1.800.423.3563
www.acei.org

Association for Behavior Analysis
1219 South Park Street
Kalamazoo, MI 49001
269.492.9310
http://www.abainternational.org

Council for Exceptional Children (CEC)
1110 North Glebe Road, Suite 300, Arlington, VA 22201
703.620.3660
TTY: 703.264.9446

FAX: 703.264.9494
E-mail: service@cec.sped.org
www.cec.sped.org

Council for Children with Behavioral Disorders
1110 North Glebe Road, Suite 300, Arlington, VA 22201
703.620.3660
www.ccbd.net

The Division for Early Childhood
634 Eddy
Missoula, Montana 59812-6696
406.243.5898
Fax 406.243.4730
Email dec@selway.umt.edu
www.dec-sped.org

National Association for the Education of Young
    Children
1509 16th Street
Washington, D.C. 20036-1426
1.800.424.2460
www.naeyc.org

Southern Early Childhood Association
8500 West Markham, Suite 105
Little Rock, AR 72204
1.800.305.7322
www.southernearlychildhood.org

Journals and Magazines

Childhood Education, Infancy through Early Adolescence
Association for the Education of Young Children

Dimensions of Early Childhood
Southern Early Childhood Association
www.southernearlychildhood.org

Early Childhood Today
Scholastic Inc.
557 Broadway
New York, NY 10012-3999

Early Childhood Education Journal
Kluwer Academic/Human Sciences Press
233 Spring Street
New York, NY 10013-1578

Journal of Applied Behavior Analysis
Society for Experimental Analysis of Behavior
Department of Human Development
University of Kansas
Lawrence, KS 66045-2133

Journal of Early Intervention
The Division for Early Childhood
634 Eddy
Missoula, Montana 59812-6696

Journal on Positive Behavioral Interventions
Pro-Ed
8700 Shoal Creek Blvd.
Austin, TX 78757

Texas Child Care
The Quarterly Journal for Caregivers Everywhere
Texas Workforce Commission
P.O. Box 162881
Austin, TX 78716-2881

Topics in Early Childhood Special Education
Pro-Ed
8700 Shoal Creek Blvd.
Austin, TX 78757

Young Children
National Association for the Education of Young
    Children
www.naeyc.org

Young Exceptional Children
The Division for Early Childhood
www.dec-sped.org

Important Websites

American Psychological Association
http://www.apa.org/
Information and contacts for psychological needs

Arizona Behavioral Initiative
http://abi.ed.asu.edu/
Resources and presentations on positive behavioral support

Arizona Positive Behavioral Support Project
http://www.nau.edu/~ihd/positive/
English and Spanish resources that explain the principles of positive behavioral support

Association for Behavior Analysis
www.abainternational.org
Searchable website on behavior analysis topics.

Beach Center on Disability
http://www.beachcenter.org
Wide variety of publications targeted toward parents of children with special needs

The Behavior Homepage: Working to make a Difference for Children who Display Challenging Behaviors
http://www.state.ky.us/agencies/behave/homepage.html
Website for school personnel, parents, and others to gain access to information, to share effective practices concerning behavior problems

Behavior Online
http://www.behavior.net/
Discussions with professionals about problem behavior

Bibliography of Positive Behavioral Support References
http://www.nichcy.org/pubs/bibliog/bib3txt.htm
Reading list for those wanting extensive knowledge of behavior supports

Center for Effective Collaboration and Practice
http://www.air.org/cecp/fba/default.htm
Resources for collaboration and problem solving to address challenging behavior

Closing the Gap
http://www.closingthegap.com
Searchable website for articles on the use of assistive technology and behavioral support.

Discipline with Dignity
http://www.disciplineassociates.com/tip.htm
Website with discipline principles for teachers

Dr. Reed Hardy
http://www.snc.edu/psych/rhar.htm
A computer-based tutorial on behavior analysis

Educational and Community Supports, University of Oregon
http://www.uoecs.org/
Resources to prevent and improve challenging behavior

ERIC Clearinghouse on Elementary and Early Childhood Education
http://www.ericeece.org/
Articles and information on educational topics regarding young children

Facilitator's Guide: Positive Behavioral Supports
http://www.fmhi.usf.edu/cfs/cfspubs/pbsguide/facilitatorguidepbs.htm
A step-by-step process to guide teams through assessment, planning, intervention, and evaluation to develop an
    understanding of circumstances affecting a student's behavior and to design interventions that lead to positive
    life-style changes

Florida's Positive Behavioral Support Project
http://www.fmhi.usf.edu/cfs/dares/flpbs/
Website for positive behavioral support for children with special needs

Functional Behavioral Assessment and Positive Behavioral Support
http://www.albany.edu/psy/autism/behavior.html
Website from the University of Albany for positive behavioral support

Indiana Resource Center for Autism
http://www.iidc.indiana.edu/irca/
Behavioral and other interventions often needed with children with autism

Online Academy of the Alabama State Department of Education
http://www.pickens.k12.al.us/Lee%20v%20Macon/behavior%20support/StartHere.htm
Resources for educating teachers and parents on positive behavior support

On-line Academy for Positive Behavioral Support

http://onlineacademy.org/

Courses offered online to teach the principles of behavior analysis and support

OSEP Technical Assistance Center of Positive Behavioral Support and Intervention

http://www.pbis.org/

Office of Special Education Programs offers information on many types of support for children with behavior
   problems

Parent Advocacy Coalition for Educational Rights

http://www.pacer.org/

A parent center that provides training and support for children with a variety of special needs

Positive Approaches to Challenging Behavior for Young Children with Disabilities

http://ici2.umn.edu/preschoolbehavior/

Website from the University of Minnesota's Center for Early Education and Development

Positive Behavioral Interventions

http://www.catchword.com/titles/10983007.htm

Articles on positive interventions to support behavioral improvement

Positive Reinforcement Tutorial

http://psych.athabascau.ca/html/prtut/reinpair.htm

A tutorial on the principles of positive reinforcement from the Psychology Department at Athabasca University

Prevention Strategies That Work

http://cecp.air.org/preventionstrategies/

Projects funded by the U.S. Department of Education, Office of Special Education Programs

Rehabilitation Research & Training Center on Positive Behavior Support

http://www.rrtcpbs.org

National research and training effort to develop and disseminate procedures for improving support for individuals
   with problem behavior

PsycLine

http://www.psycline.org/

Enables you to research behavioral issues in journals by keyword

Dr. Tim Lewis

www.missouri.edu/~spedtl/

Website with Dr. Lewis' presentations and information on positive behavioral support

Western Regional Resource Center

http://interact.uoregon.edu/WRRC/Behavior.html#FBA\

Website from the University of Oregon on challenging behavior

Wisconsin Department of Public Instruction: Behavioral Interventions

http://www.pickens.k12.al.us/Lee%20v%20Macon/behavior%20support/StartHere.htm

Online academy with modules designed to teach validated educational interventions for children with problem
behavior

References

Alberto, P.A., & A.C. Troutman. 2002. *Applied behavior analysis for teachers.* Upper Saddle River, NJ: Prentice Hall.

Bodrova, E. and D. Leong. 1995. *Tools of the mind: The Vygotskian approach to early childhood education.* Englewood Cliffs, New Jersey: Prentice Hall.

Bredekamp, S. & C. Copple, Eds. 1997. *Developmentally appropriate practice in early childhood programs* (revised ed). Washington, DC: National Association for the Education of Young Children.

Connell, M. C., J.J. Carta, & D.M. Baer. 1993. Programming generalization of in-class transition skills: Teaching preschoolers with developmental disabilities to self-assess and recruit contingent teacher praise. *Journal of Applied Behavior Analysis,* 26(2), 345-352.

Cooper, J.O., T.E. Heron, & W.L. Heward. 1987. *Applied behavior analysis.* Upper Saddle River, NJ: Prentice Hall.

Davis, C. A., & J. Reichle. 1996. Variant and invariant high-probability requests: Increasing appropriate behaviors in children with emotional behavioral disorders. *Journal of Applied Behavior Analysis,* 29, 471-481.

Dunn, W. 1999. *Sensory profile user's manual.* San Antonio, TX: The Psychological Corporation.

Durand, V. M. 1990. *Severe behavior problems: A functional communication training approach.* New York: Guilford.

Fulghum, R. 1987. *All I ever needed to know I learned in kindergarten.* New York: Ballantine.

Gray, C. 2000. *The new social story book: Illustrated edition.* Arlington, TX: Future Horizons.

Hendrick, J. 2002. *Total learning, developmental curriculum for the young child (6th ed.).* Columbus, OH: Prentice Hall.

Joseph, G.E. & P.S. Strain. 2003. Helping young children control anger and disappointment. *Young Exceptional Children,* 7(1), 21-29.

Kaplan, J.S. 1995. *Beyond behavior modification: A cognitive behavioral approach to behavior management in the school (3rd ed.).* Austin, TX: Pro-Ed.

Katz, L. & D. McClelland. 1997. *Fostering children's social competence: The Teacher's Role.* Washington, DC: National Association for the Education of Young Children.

Kauffman, J.M. 2001. *Characteristics of emotional and behavioral disorders of children and youth (7th Ed.).* Upper Saddle River, NJ: Prentice Hall.

Maag, J.W. 2004. *Behavior management: From theoretical implications to practical applications (2nd ed.)*. Belmont, CA: Thomson/Wadsworth.

Maag, J. W. 1999. *Behavior management: From theoretical implications to practical applications*. San Diego, CA: Singular Publishing Group.

Manolson, A. 1992. *It takes two to talk: A parent's guide to helping children communicate (3rd ed.)*. Toronto, Ontario: The Hanen Centre.

Montessori, M. 1965. *Dr. Montessori's own handbook*. New York: Schocken.

Morrison, G. S. 2004. *Early childhood education today (9th ed.)*. Upper Saddle River, NJ: Pearson Prentice Hall.

O'Neill, R.,R. Horner, R. Albin, J. Sprague, K. Storey, & J.S. Newton. 1997. *Functional assessment and program development for problem behavior: A practical handbook (2nd ed.)*. Pacific Grove, CA: Brooks/Cole Publishing Company.

Orem, R. 1974. *Montessori, her method and the movement: What you need to know*. New York: Putnam.

Premack, D. 1959. Toward empirical behavior laws: I. Positive reinforcement. *Psychological Review*, 66, 219-233.

Schneider, M. 1974. Turtle technique in the classroom. *Young Exceptional Children*, 7(1), 21-24.

Standing, E. 1984. *Maria Montessori, her life and work*. London: New American Library.

Walker, H. M., R.H. Horner, G. Sugai, M. Bullis, J.R. Sprague, D. Bricker, & M.J. Kaufman. 1996. Integrated approaches to preventing anti-social behavior among school-age children and youth. *Journal of Emotional and Behavioral Disorders*, 4(4), 194-209.

White, O. R. & N.G. Haring. 1976. *Exceptional teaching*. Upper Saddle River, NJ: Prentice Hall.

Index

Children's Book Index